KU-746-802

Book No. **02657359**

30121 0 02657359

Britain's Shadow Economy

Britain's Shadow Economy

STEPHEN SMITH

The Institute for Fiscal Studies
London

CLARENDON PRESS . OXFORD
1986

STAFFORDSHIRE
POLYTECHNIC
LIBRARY

Oxford University Press, Walton Street, Oxford OX2 6DP.

Oxford New York Toronto
Delhi Bombay Calcutta Madras Karachi
Petaling Jaya Singapore Hong Kong Tokyo
Nairobi Dar es Salaam Cape Town
Melbourne Auckland
and associated companies in
Beirut Berlin Ibadan Nicosia

Oxford is a trade mark of Oxford University Press

Published in the United States
by Oxford University Press, New York

© The Institute for Fiscal Studies, 1986

All rights reserved. No part of this publication may be reproduced, stored in a retrieval
system, or transmitted, in any form or by any means, electronic, mechanical, photocopying,
recording, or otherwise, without the prior permission of Oxford University Press

This book is sold subject to the condition that it shall not, by way of trade or otherwise, be
lent, re-sold, hired out or otherwise circulated without the publisher's prior consent in any
form of binding or cover other than that in which it is published and without a similar
condition including this condition being imposed on the subsequent purchaser

British Library Cataloguing in Publication Data
Smith, Stephen
Britain's shadow economy
1. Tax evasion—Great Britain
I. Title
364.1'33   HJ2348.5
ISBN 0-19-828569-8

Library of Congress Cataloging in Publication Data
Smith, Stephen
Britain's shadow economy
1. Informal sector (Economics)—Great Britain
I. Title
HD2346.G7S65   1986   381   86-16352
ISBN 0-19-828569-8

Typeset from disk by Parchment (Oxford) Ltd, Oxford

Printed in Great Britain
at the University Printing House, Oxford
by David Stanford
Printer to the University

STAFFORDSHIRE
POLYTECHNIC

2 3 MAY 1990

CLASS No.
364·133

02657359

Preface

This book has developed out of a joint research project into the shadow economy in Britain and West Germany, undertaken by the Institute for Fiscal Studies and the Institute für Angewandte Wirtschaftsforschung (IAW), Tübingen, West Germany. The results of the comparative study of Britain and West Germany are being published by the Anglo-German Foundation, which sponsored the research. However, during the course of the project it was decided that some aspects of the UK research were being developed in considerably greater detail than would be appropriate for the comparative volume, and that the UK research merited publication in its own right. This book is the result.

Despite the single-country focus of this book, the author has benefited considerably from the broader perspective encouraged by the Anglo-German project. Discussions with the researchers at IAW—Günther Petry and Susanne Wied-Nebbeling—have been particularly valuable, and the author is also grateful for the interest and support of Barbara Beck and Hans Wiener of the Anglo-German Foundation.

Two of the chapters in the book are the result of joint endeavour: Michael Kell worked with the author on Chapter 10, 'Evidence from the Demand for Cash', and Chris Pissarides and Guglielmo Weber contributed to Chapter 12, 'Evidence from Survey Discrepancies'. The author is grateful for their advice and assistance. In addition, many others have provided helpful comments, especially Richard Clare and Nick Coote at the CSO. They are, of course, in no way responsible for any errors that remain.

The author would like to thank Chantal Crevel-Robinson, Alice Terrell, and Siân Turner, who have patiently typed successive drafts of the manuscript, and Judith Payne, for the great care she has taken in copy-editing the text for publication.

Contents

List of figures

List of tables

STAFFORDSHIRE
POLYTECHNIC
LIBRARY

Part I
Introduction

Chapter 1

Introduction

Increasing academic attention has been focused on the notion of a 'hidden' economy, operating in the shadow of the formal, measured economy. One part of this economy is economic activity hidden because it is illegal (the drug trade, employee theft, etc.). Other activity may have been concealed to avoid paying tax, or to establish a false entitlement to social security benefits. This is the so-called 'black economy'. A still wider group of activities remain unmeasured despite not being deliberately concealed. Nearly all the productive activities that go on within households, for example, escape measurement in the national accounts, and have as a result been largely ignored by economic analysis.

The 'shadow economy', the subject of this book, includes all of these activities. It embraces a range of extremely varied phenomena. At one extreme the shadow economy includes the black economy of moonlighting, tax-dodging, and 'scrounging'. At the other end of the spectrum it extends to such familiar, and innocuous, household activities as washing up, baby-sitting, and do-it-yourself (DIY) home improvements. The economic context of such activities, the factors that influence them, and their relevance for economic policy-making all vary widely.

One might reasonably wonder what point there is in drawing together such a variety of different activities under the same heading, and what could be gained from analysing them together. The question of the appropriate tax enforcement policy to combat the black economy, for example, seems to have no public policy counterpart in relation to the unpaid domestic work of housewives, and lumping the two activities together under the same heading would seem to create more confusion than clarity. Often, indeed, this will be so, and in this book the constituent parts of the shadow economy are, in the main, considered separately. Parts II and III, for example, concentrate on the black economy, while Part IV is devoted to the wider shadow economy of unpaid housework, voluntary work in the community, and so forth. Nevertheless, there are common themes and common issues that arise.

One is the issue of *measurement*. Neither the black economy nor the wider range of shadow economy activities including DIY, housework, and voluntary work is reflected to any great extent in the national accounts. The statistics of gross domestic product (GDP) and of national income are almost entirely confined to production and factor incomes arising in the formal economy, where transactions are subject to tax and can be given a straightforward monetary valuation. The reasons that the constituent parts of the shadow economy are not measured in the national accounts differ. In the case of the black economy it is because the activities are concealed. Other shadow economy activities are quite open, but are omitted from the national accounts by definition. Nevertheless, the issue of how much higher gross domestic product would be if all economic activity were included in the national accounts is one question that unites the different strands of the shadow economy.

Estimates that have been made of the scale of the shadow economy suggest that parts of the shadow economy at least may be very significant in relation to measured gross domestic product. Hawrylyshyn (1976), for example, summarises a considerable number of estimates of the value of unpaid production activity in households in the United States; these suggest that the value of such production might be equivalent to some 30 to 40 per cent of US gross domestic product. Estimates of the size of the black economy are much more controversial. Feige (1980) has argued that in 1979 the black economy in the US was equivalent to 27 per cent of the formal economy, as measured by official statistics, but a study by the US Internal Revenue Service (1979), based on intensive audit of a sample of taxpayers, concludes with a less fantastic estimate that some 6 per cent of taxable income was not reported to the tax authorities. The range of estimates of the size of the UK black economy extends from about 2 per cent of GDP (Dilnot and Morris, 1981) to about 15 per cent (Matthews and Rastogi, 1985). The 'official' view, as put by Sir William Pile, then Chairman of the Board of Inland Revenue, at a hearing of the House of Commons Expenditure Committee (1979), is that it was 'not implausible' that incomes not declared for tax could amount to $7\frac{1}{2}$ per cent of national income.

Some authors have argued that if the black economy is as large as some of these figures suggest, much of our present economic malaise may simply be an illusion generated by our reliance on statistics of the formal economy to interpret overall economic conditions. Growth may in fact be higher, and inflation and unemployment lower, than the official statistics suggest. Gutmann (1979a), for example, has referred to the unemployment 'illusion', and Matthews (1983) has contended that as many as 1.3 million of the 3 million UK unemployed in 1983 may in fact have been actively employed in the black economy.

It is hardly surprising that such startling and controversial claims should have received considerable media attention. The 'story' has of course many of the ingredients likely to whet the tabloid appetite: 'scroungers' and 'fiddlers'; the avaricious taxman; the injustice suffered by the law-abiding majority (minority?); and so on. It is unfortunate, but perhaps predictable, that other more sceptical studies have attracted less publicity. Tanzi's (1982) conclusion—that belief in a black economy in excess of 8 per cent of GDP must be based on 'faith rather than reason'—has failed to have the impact that such a careful review of the evidence deserves.

The nature of the phenomenon itself fosters the production of widely diverging estimates of the scale of the black economy. Since many of the participants in the black economy have reason to conceal what they are doing, measurement will always be difficult, and even the most careful study will be unlikely to convince those persuaded of the opposite point of view. For the same reason, wild and improbable estimates are peculiarly difficult to refute. The criteria for evaluating research results in this area are less obvious than in others, and the subject is bedevilled too by the intrusive political and moral views of some of the participants in the debate.

Achieving greater precision in the estimates of the size of the various parts of the shadow economy is, in itself, a useful statistical exercise. A number of different routes to assessing the size of the black economy are explored in Chapters 9 to 12 in Part III, while Chapter 14 considers how the wider shadow economy, including household production, might be measured.

Nevertheless, the central issue for public policy is not so much the size of the shadow economy, or of its constituent parts, but rather the extent of *substitution* between the formal economy and the shadow economy. It is the possibility that the shadow economy may be growing at the expense of the formal economy that prompts concern about the adequacy of official statistics for macroeconomic management. Similarly, it is the possibility that taxation and the pattern of tax enforcement activities may be encouraging substitution away from efficient patterns of economic activity towards less efficient, but untaxed, patterns of activity that gives rise to the most pressing questions about tax enforcement.

Sometimes the debate over measurement of shadow economy activities in the national accounts is put in terms of the 'incompleteness' of existing measurement methods. We need a new basis for national accounting, so the argument goes, because productive activities in households and by tax evaders are not reflected in the existing national accounts statistics. It is certainly true that if the national accounts are used as an indicator of long-term trends in living standards, or to compare living standards between countries, then there are problems of omission. But in the main application for which modern national accounts statistics have been designed—as indicators of macroeconomic trends to be used in the formulation of macroeconomic policy—the incomplete coverage of these statistics may be less of a problem. What would be a problem is if the border-line between the shadow economy and the formal economy were unstable, with substantial substitution from one to the other over time. Then the rate of growth of the formal economy, measured by official statistics, might bear little relation to the rate of growth of the overall economy, and the usefulness of official statistics for macroeconomic management would be limited.

Substitution is important too in policy towards taxation. The Inland Revenue's estimate that the black economy amounts to some $7\frac{1}{2}$ per cent of GDP might appear to imply a substantial loss of tax revenue. It is by no means clear, however, that all of this 'lost' revenue could—or should—be recovered by devoting more resources to enforcement by the Inland Revenue. Much would depend on how people with sources of black economy income would choose to react if they knew that any income they earned would be subject to tax. Some might decide that they would rather not work so hard if they were going to be taxed on the resulting income. If many people reacted in this way, enforcement would yield little revenue, because the substitution back to the formal economy would be small; and the loss of output as a result of enforcement would be large. Alternatively, devoting more resources to enforcement might encourage substitution back to the formal economy, and might yield benefits in terms of overall economic efficiency—for example, by ensuring that honest, efficient firms were no longer undercut by their dishonest, less efficient rivals. Adjusting tax policy to the precise characteristics of individual cases is, of course, rarely practicable. However, enforcement is clearly a matter of choosing priorities; and perhaps some classes of tax evaders should be pursued with more vigour than others. The ease of substitution between the formal and shadow economies will be an important element in making these choices.

The outline of this book is as follows. In the remainder of Part I, Chapter 2 covers issues of definition, and Chapter 3 describes the relationship between the shadow economy and the UK national accounts. Part II looks at the possible influences on the level and growth of the black economy in the UK, including tax and benefit rates, enforcement policy, and the opportunities for tax evasion and benefit fraud. Part III discusses how the black economy might be measured, examining three possible approaches in detail in Chapters 10 to 12. Part IV considers the wider shadow economy, especially housework and DIY. Chapter 14 discusses how it might be measured, and Chapter 15 investigates the scope for substitutions between the formal economy and the shadow economy in a number of areas. Chapter 16, in Part V, draws some conclusions.

Chapter 2

Defining the shadow economy

A plethora of names have been coined to refer to the shadow economy, or to parts of it. Writers in the English language have referred to the hidden economy, black, grey, twilight or shadow economies, a parallel, underground or subterranean economy, the cash economy, and so forth. A similar quest for a euphonious term or a snappy characterisation has been evident in the literature in other languages.

The variety of terms used to describe aspects of the shadow economy has unfortunately tended to obscure some important distinctions between the economic and social phenomena involved. On the one hand, writers have often used different terms for the same phenomenon; on the other hand, similar terms have been used with rather different meanings. All too often, definitional issues have been side-stepped by the adoption of a different term, and differences in meaning or definition have been ignored rather than emphasised.

We do not intend here to try to unravel the tangled web of vague, overlapping, and in places contradictory meanings that previous studies have attached to the terms they have used. Rather, this chapter aims to explain clearly the two main terms that are used in this study, to draw attention to possible sources of ambiguity, and to indicate how the terms interrelate. Broadly speaking, the two terms used are defined in the following way. The *'shadow economy'* is defined as including all economic activity that is not recorded in the national accounts, including productive activities in households and voluntary organisations, as well as the unreported and unrecorded economic activity associated with tax evasion and benefit fraud. The term *'black economy'* is used in a narrower sense, covering economic activity that is accompanied by tax evasion or benefit fraud, or that is concealed because it is illegal. The shadow economy thus includes the black economy, but goes much wider.

6

The basis for definition

Two broad themes underlie the notion of a hidden, black, or shadow economy, and either could be chosen as the basis for a consistent set of definitions and terminology. The first of these—the issue of the extent of *tax evasion*—seems to lie at the heart of what is popularly meant by the 'black economy'. Earnings in the black economy are earnings on which taxes should be paid but are not. The second notion is that of *unrecorded activity*: the 'shadow economy' is that portion of economic activity that, for one reason or another, fails to be recorded in official statistics such as gross national product or national income.

The two are of course closely linked. Economic activity that is concealed from the eyes of the taxman may also escape the notice of official statisticians, especially if tax returns are one of the primary data sources used to estimate income statistics. Conditions that give rise to increased tax evasion will then also tend to increase the extent of unrecorded national income.

Nevertheless, as Feige has written:

One of the major ambiguities which has plagued the literature on the underground economy has been the repeated confusion between economic and fiscal concepts of income. All too often tax evasion has been erroneously identified with unrecorded income in NIPAs [national accounts] ... 'Unreported fiscal income' is a totally different concept than 'unrecorded economic income'. The former represents an empirical understatement of total taxable income, whereas the latter reflects an underestimation of total economic income.
(Feige, 1985)

The policy issues raised by the shadow economy reflect these two different analytical orientations. On the one hand, the amount of tax revenue lost through unreported taxable income may be a matter for concern. There are a set of important policy questions about the level of resources that it is desirable to devote to combating tax evasion and benefit fraud. Equally, a different set of policy issues are raised if changes in the shadow economy lead to a deterioration in the reliability of the statistical indicators—gross domestic product (GDP), the unemployment rate, the inflation rate, and so on—that form the basis for macroeconomic policymaking. If growing tax evasion leads national income accountants to under-estimate the true level of personal income in

GDP (because they rely on tax data for much of their information about personal incomes), or if growing benefit fraud means that the published unemployment figures exceed the number of people who are genuinely out of work, then policymakers may be induced to take inappropriate action, to cure non-existent macroeconomic ills.

Both these sets of issues are worth debating. As far as possible, the terminology used in this book aims to facilitate discussion of both the extent of tax evasion and the extent to which the shadow economy may be omitted from statistics of national income and output. The description 'black economy' is used to refer to economic activity on which tax is evaded or that is concealed because it is illegal, whilst the term 'shadow economy' is used to cover a wider range of economic activities not measured by the national accounts. Both terms, however, should be understood to refer to the amount of economic activity involved, so that, for example, the size of the black economy is the amount of factor income on which tax is evaded, rather than the amount of tax that is not paid. In this sense, the main focus of the terminology is the measurement and recording of economic activity. Where the amount of tax lost through tax evasion is at issue, this is made explicit.

Definitions of terms used

Figure 2.1 gives an overview of the terms used in this book, and indicates how the shadow economy and the black economy are related, both to each other and to the notions of 'market' and 'non-market' economic activity. It also gives a preliminary indication—pending the more detailed discussion in the next chapter—of the extent to which the various kinds of economic activity are included in the UK national accounts figures for gross domestic product. Figure 2.2 shows some examples of the activities that are included in the various parts of the shadow economy.

Total economic activity is divided into economic activity in the 'formal economy' and in the 'shadow economy'. The formal economy comprises both the above-board, recorded market transactions of individual companies and other institutions, and a considerable amount of non-marketed economic activity, mainly the spending of central government and local authorities on roads,

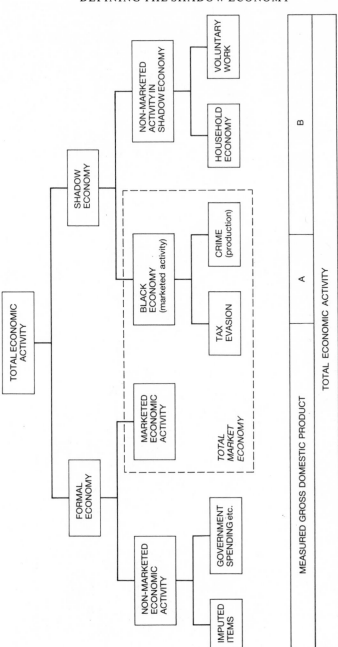

A – Activities that should, in principle, be measured in GDP, but are not because they are hidden.
B – Activities excluded from GDP by convention.

FIGURE 2.1

Relationships Within the Formal and Shadow Economies

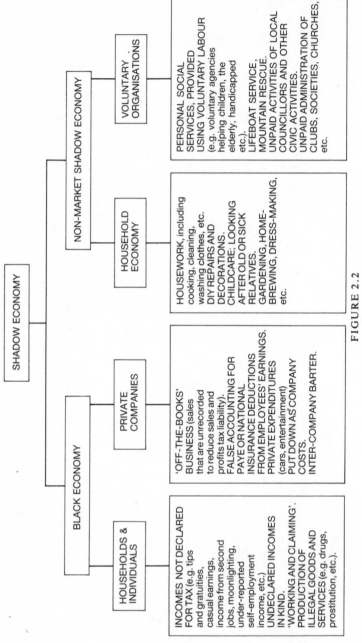

FIGURE 2.2

Examples of Activity in the Shadow Economy

education, health, defence, and so on. The formal economy might loosely be described as the 'measured economy', in that its boundaries are largely coextensive with those of measured gross domestic product.

The 'shadow economy' too contains both marketed and non-marketed activities. The market activities within the shadow economy are described as the 'black economy', and comprise economic activity on which tax is evaded and the production of illegal goods and services. The non-market activities within the shadow economy comprise both the production of goods and services within households (cooking, childcare, do-it-yourself, etc.) and the activities of voluntary organisations. Examples are shown in Figure 2.2.

A satisfactory generic term for the non-market shadow economy is hard to find. Some of the terms that have been suggested, including the 'non-profit economy' or the 'self-service economy', seem not to reflect the full scope of the activities involved or their difference from other non-market activities in the formal economy.

There are two areas of ambiguity in these definitions. The first is in the precise relationship between the shadow economy/formal economy border-line and the boundaries of the 'measured economy' reflected in the UK national accounts. The second is in the degree of precision that can be given to the relationship between economic activity in the black economy and tax evasion.

The formal economy, as defined above, is much the same as the economic activity measured in the UK national accounts; the shadow economy, therefore, corresponds largely to those activities not included in the national accounts. This division is not always straightforward, and the appropriate place within this framework for the imputed items in the national accounts is unclear. These imputed items include estimated amounts for the imputed rent from owner-occupied houses, and certain forms of income-in-kind such as company cars, free meals, and so forth.

As will be clear from the discussion of imputation in the next chapter, the number and value of imputed items in the UK accounts are not large, and the basis on which items are chosen for imputation is pragmatic rather than based on a clear conceptual framework. Some writers would put most of the imputed items with the shadow economy, and given the rather arbitrary way in which items are chosen for imputation this is perhaps the most

STAFFORDSHIRE
POLYTECHNIC
LIBRARY

consistent approach. In Figure 2.1, however, they are shown as part of the non-marketed economic activity within the formal economy, increasing the extent to which the formal and measured economies coincide.

A similar issue arises over the treatment of the estimated amounts included in the UK national accounts for economic activity on which tax is evaded. If the distinguishing characteristic of the shadow economy is that it is not measured in gross domestic product, then, arguably, part at least of the economic activity of moonlighters and other tax evaders should not be included in the shadow economy. The estimated level of income on which tax is evaded would then be included in the formal economy; only if the actual level of tax evasion exceeded the 'evasion adjustment' in the national accounts would any economic activity associated with tax evasion be included in the shadow economy. If we then define the 'black economy' as including all economic activity on which tax is evaded, then part or all of the black economy may in fact be measured in the national accounts, and hence lie outside the shadow economy.

Normal usage, however, is at odds with this approach, and it is not adopted here. Instead, the shadow economy is defined to cover *all* of the black economy, including all tax-evaded incomes, regardless of whether any estimates of tax-evaded incomes have been included in the national accounts. Part of the shadow economy may thus be reflected in the national accounts, to the extent that income items are adjusted for possible evasion. This approach does involve a certain heterogeneity in the definition of the shadow economy, since it can no longer be defined neatly as those items that are not measured in the national accounts, but it does have the advantage of defining the shadow economy in a way that is less dependent on the precise methods used to adjust the UK national accounts for tax evasion.

The second main area of ambiguity in the definitions of the terms used in this study is in the boundary of the black economy. How much tax evasion does there have to be for an activity to be part of the black economy? Popular usage provides some clear examples of what might be included. People who do not declare income for tax on casual jobs or occasional self-employed work in their spare time, repairing cars, or painting and decorating, are generally regarded as working in the black economy. Similarly, unemployed people who are earning money for occasional work, or who indeed may have a full-time job at the same time as they are claiming unemployment benefit, also fall into the black economy category. But some other cases are less clear. If the local butcher's van is running with an out-of-date tax disk, is the butcher's turn-over to be counted as part of the black economy? For absolute consistency, perhaps it should be. But there is clearly a world of difference between an out-of-date tax disk (whether accidental or intentional) and more substantial cases of tax evasion which may significantly affect the pattern of competition between producers.

Ultimately, the activities included in the black economy will be those where the tax evasion is significant, either in the sense that it is large enough to affect the pattern of competition between 'honest' businesses and those evading tax, or in the sense that it is likely in other ways to involve effort being devoted to substitution away from the taxed sector. Thus, for example, if the butcher's van runs with an out-of-date tax disk we would not count his turn-over as part of the black economy, but if a car-hire firm taxed none of its cars, and was thereby able to offer especially low rates, we would. In practice, in this book, discussion of the black economy is largely confined to a limited number of major taxes—value added tax, income tax, National Insurance contributions—and the problems of unemployment benefit abuse, where tax evasion could conceivably have significant effects in this sense.

Chapter 3

The shadow economy and the national accounts

The national income accounts measure the money value of goods and services becoming available to the nation from economic activity, or equivalently the incomes of corporate and individual residents of the nation that are derived from economic activity. The incomes that count are the incomes of factors of production, or 'factor incomes'. Transfer payments for which no goods or services are received in return, such as pensions, social security and gifts, are not included in the national income total. They do not increase the total spending power of the economy, but merely transfer spending power from one person to another.

Most of the shadow economy does not appear in the national accounts. Indeed, some authors have *defined* the shadow economy as those activities that are not measured in the national accounts statistics. MacAfee (1980), for example, defines the hidden economy as 'the economic activity generating factor incomes which cannot be estimated from the regular statistical sources used to compile the income measure of gross domestic product'.

There are two main reasons that activity in the shadow economy may be excluded from the national income accounts. Firstly, some of the activities, such as housework, that are included in the shadow economy fall outside the definition of 'economic activity' used in the national accounts. Secondly, other activities that in principle ought to be included in the national accounts may be missed out, or alternatively may be simply guessed, because of a lack of information about their extent. The importance of each of these sources of omission is considered in the following two sections.

Issues of definition

The definition of economic activity used in the UK national

accounts is narrower in scope than the broad definition used here. Little of the productive economic activity within the household economy is reflected in the UK national accounts. These accounts are largely confined to measuring the traded goods and services produced by industry, and the economic activity of central and local government.

The choice of this comparatively restricted definition of 'economic activity' for the UK national accounts is based largely on pragmatic considerations, and is closely bound up with how easily different activities can be measured. The output of industry can be straightforwardly valued by the prices at which its products are sold in the market-place, and the factor incomes corresponding to industrial output can be assessed from statistics of wages paid and profits earned. Non-marketed production, such as the 'output' of the health service or of the army, cannot be valued from the output side. Nevertheless, an estimate of its value can be made from the input side, by calculating the costs of inputs, including factor incomes, and such an estimate is included in the UK national accounts.

But measurement difficulties become more acute where neither the inputs nor the output of some activity are subject to a market valuation. The domestic services of housewives, and householders' do-it-yourself decoration and home improvements, for example, are not exchanged for money, and the value given to them would be considerably more arbitrary than the values given to the outputs of traded goods and services. As the Central Statistical Office (CSO) puts it:

In computing a money measure of the nation's production, it is most convenient to confine attention to activities yielding goods and services which can be given a value which is not wholly arbitrary. This means substantially those goods and services which are in fact exchanged for money.
(Maurice, 1968, p. 7)

Drawing the boundary of 'economic activity' at this point may have advantages in making measurement comparatively straightforward. But it may produce anomalies if there is a possibility of substitution over time between marketed and non-marketed 'production'. Generations of economics students are familiar with the textbook example of how national income is reduced if a man marries his housekeeper. As a paid housekeeper her services are reflected in the national accounts, but as an unpaid housewife the same services go unrecorded. While a few marriages of this sort are unlikely to distort the estimates of national income significantly, there may be some less trivial possibilities of substitution which could have an effect on national income comparisons made over time or between countries. Partly for this reason, the UK statistics extend a little beyond the boundary of marketed production to cover certain kinds of activity that are not actually exchanged for money.

The principal example is the rent imputed in the UK national accounts to the owners of owner-occupied houses. No money actually passes between the owner and the occupier of a house when they are the same person. Nevertheless, the services of the building can be viewed as having a value equivalent to the net rental income that could be obtained by letting the building commercially. The owner-occupier of the house is treated, for national accounts purposes, as two separate people: as owner he lets the house to himself at a market rent. (Until 1963 a similar imputed income of owner-occupiers was calculated by the Inland Revenue and taxed under Schedule A.) The allowance made in the UK national accounts for the imputed rent of owner-occupied dwellings amounts to some 4 per cent of gross domestic product (GDP).

There are, in addition, a few other, less significant, cases of imputation in the UK national accounts, generally where 'a reasonably satisfactory basis for the assumed valuation is available' (Maurice, 1968). In general, these cases are those where the imputed transactions are closely similar to other transactions in which money actually changes hands, i.e. where the goods and services involved are those that are 'customarily exchanged for money' (Maurice, 1968). Amounts are imputed for the benefits that employees derive from company cars and fuel, and also for some small amounts of income-in-kind, including the free coal provided to miners and the free meals and accommodation enjoyed by some employees. These imputed items are included in the national income figures for income from employment, and amount in total to less than 1 per cent of GDP.

The arguments against extending the scope of imputation are principally to do with the measurement difficulties involved. It is recognised that the fact that the unpaid activities of housewives are excluded from national income will make comparison of national income over time misleading if the amount of work done by housewives varies substantially over time. Similarly, since no amount is imputed for the services provided by consumer durable goods such as washing machines and motor cars, the measure of national income takes no account of the fact that the benefits from owning a car or a washing machine may be spread over a number of years after purchase. If, during a recession, people temporarily reduce their purchases of new durables, they may nonetheless continue to use their existing assets. Their standard of living may therefore fall considerably less than the fall in their purchases of durables would suggest.

Comparisons of economic activity between countries may also be distorted by differences in the balance of market and non-market economic activity. Building one's own house is rare in the United Kingdom, but more common in less developed countries and in some industrial countries. Subsistence agricultural production too is comparatively unimportant in the UK, but may be of greater significance in countries where the agricultural sector contains more small firms and small holdings. The UN–OECD System of National Accounts (SNA) aims to achieve some consistency in the coverage of the national accounts of different countries, though the extent of imputation under SNA rules is still comparatively small, and comparisons of different countries' accounts based on SNA will generally be affected by different boundaries between market and non-market activity. Generally, gross domestic product estimated according to SNA rules excludes virtually all of the economic activity of the 'household economy' with the exception of building and improving dwellings, the housing services that owner-occupiers provide for themselves, and subsistence activities undertaken in farm households (Blades, 1982).

Under the SNA rules, factor incomes arising from illegal activity would be included in the estimation of gross domestic product. Few countries make any explicit allowance for illegal activities in their national accounts. Blades (1982) reports that of the OECD countries only the US and Italy make estimates of illegal production; in both cases the amounts involved are trivial and cover only a small part of illegal activity.

Not everyone would agree that illegal activity should be included in national income statistics. The notion that a country may be held to be better off the higher the level of illegal activity seems unsatisfactory, and the idea that national income statistics should appear to attribute benefits to heroin trafficking, for example, may seem repugnant. On the other hand there appears to be no dispute that certain kinds of illegal activity should be reflected in the national accounts. The factor incomes earned from Sunday trading, for example, are presumably included in the UK's gross domestic product without reference to the laws governing Sunday trading. Indeed, it would seem desirable that for many of the applications for which national accounts statistics are used—for macroeconomic forecasting, for example—all factor incomes should be included, regardless of their legal status. That no allowance is made in the UK national accounts for the factor incomes from concealed criminal activities is perhaps something that might reasonably reflect the measurement difficulties involved, but not any issue of principle.

Omissions due to concealed or unrecorded incomes

Besides those parts of the shadow economy that are not included in the national accounts as a matter of definition, some economic activity in the shadow economy may fail to be reflected in the national accounts because of difficulties in measurement. This is likely to be a particular problem in those parts of the shadow economy involving tax evasion, because economic activity that has been successfully concealed from the taxman may also escape the notice of the national accounts statistician. This is particularly likely where the raw data used as the basis for national accounts estimates are derived from the operation of the tax system.

The Inland Revenue is the main source of data used by the CSO to calculate the income measure of GDP in the national accounts. Estimates of the largest component—wages and salaries from employment—are compiled from Pay-As-You-Earn tax forms prepared by employers, and the estimates of self-employment incomes take as a starting point the incomes reported to the Inland Revenue by the self-employed. Companies' gross trading profits, too, are based on accounts submitted to the Inland Revenue by UK companies. In all of the cases, there is in principle a risk that incomes may have been understated in order to evade tax. Relying on these sources to estimate national income may mean that national income is under-estimated.

It by no means follows, however, that because some of the data sources used to calculate the UK national accounts statistics are affected by tax evasion, the errors in these data sources will feed through into corresponding errors in the published figures for gross domestic product and other national accounts aggregates. National accounts estimation in the UK, as in many other countries, has become an extremely complex process, incorporating a series of cross-checks on the accuracy of the estimates that are made. Gross domestic product, for example, can be estimated in three largely independent ways, only one of which—the income measure—is based to any significant extent on data derived from income tax records. The existence of alternative data sources means that it is possible to choose ways of calculating the national accounts that are affected as little as possible by evasion (although, as Chapter 11 notes, all may be affected to some extent by evasion). It may also, indeed, make it possible to estimate the relative extent to which different data sources are affected by evasion, and hence to gauge the extent of evasion.

An example may serve to illustrate how the choice of data sources and measurement methods can help to minimise the problems caused by the under-reporting of incomes to the tax authorities. In the UK national accounts, the factor incomes from private capital invested in industry are reflected in GDP as part of company profits, which are measured gross of interest and dividend payments. No use is made of the information in individual tax returns about receipts of interest and dividends when GDP is calculated. The information on company profits is believed to be largely accurate, and the fact that some people in receipt of interest and dividends from private companies fail to declare it to the tax authorities does not affect the measurement of GDP.

Based partly on information derived from the cross-checking between different data sources, adjustments are made in the UK national accounts for income under-reporting. These vary from year to year, and are also subject to revision, depending on changes in the initial residual difference. The adjustments made to UK gross domestic product in 1980–2 are shown in Table 3.1. The adjustments are particularly substantial in the case of self-employment income, where they amounted to about one-seventh of the published item. The adjustments to employment income and to company profits are much smaller. Overall, the evasion adjustment added about 1.5 per cent to GDP.

TABLE 3.1

Evasion Adjustments to Income Items in the UK National Accounts, Average of Adjustments Made, 1980–2

	Evasion adjustment (£ million)	Published item (£ million)	Adjustment as percentage of published item (%)
Income from self-employment	2,700	19,000	14
Income from employment	} 500	148,000	} 0.3
Company profits		31,000	
GDP	*3,200*	*218,000*	*1.5*

MacAfee (1980) has described the methods used by the CSO to make these estimates. The adjustment process starts by examining the difference between GDP calculated from expenditure statistics and GDP calculated from income statistics. In theory the gap between these two—the 'initial residual difference'—should in the absence of tax evasion be zero, though in practice for statistical reasons the two methods of calculating GDP are rarely likely to give the same result. Tax evasion, however, will lead to the income measure of GDP being under-recorded, whilst the expenditure-based measure is, according to MacAfee, less likely to be affected. The initial residual difference, then, will contain two components: a random component reflecting statistical error, and a systematic component reflecting the extent to which tax evasion has led to an understatement of incomes reported to the Inland Revenue.

The evidence that the initial residual difference (IRD) gives about the size of tax evasion is considered in more detail in Chapter 11. It would appear that what had seemed to be a systematic upward trend in the IRD during the 1970s has since been reversed, and that, if anything, the IRD might now point to tax evasion on a smaller scale than is allowed for in the present GDP estimates. Nevertheless, it is clear that the CSO has taken a cautious view of the relevance of the IRD to the evasion estimates, and has tried to look for independent evidence of evasions, including advice from other government departments, such as the Inland Revenue, and evidence from production accounts.

Part II
Tax evasion and benefit fraud

Chapter 4

Introduction and theory

Tax evasion and benefit fraud usually involve telling lies, or at any rate concealing the truth from the taxman or benefit officials. Often, but not always, the information that is concealed is information about economic activity—about income or sales that would otherwise be subject to tax, or that would disqualify the claimant from receiving benefit. In other cases, however, the information that is misrepresented may be about something other than economic activity. An income tax payer, for example, may falsely claim to be married in order to receive higher allowances against tax; supplementary benefit recipients may falsely claim to be separated in order to receive benefit to which they would otherwise not be entitled.

Where taxpayers conceal income or where companies conceal profits this is likely to be reflected in the statistics of aggregate income and company profits declared for tax purposes compiled by the Inland Revenue and used as the basis for the income estimate of gross domestic product. There is thus likely to be a direct relationship between the amount of income tax and corporation tax evasion and possible errors in national accounts aggregates. Where economic activity is concealed in the evasion of other taxes, there is no necessary reason that this might feed through into national accounts errors, because information from the administration of other taxes is not routinely used in compiling the statistics of national income and gross domestic product. Similarly, if people claiming state benefits conceal income from the benefit authorities, this will not necessarily mean that the concealed income is omitted from the national accounts. Only if the income concealed from the benefit authorities is also concealed from the Inland Revenue will it normally fail to be registered in the national accounts.

It is quite likely that incomes successfully concealed from the benefit authorities are also concealed from the Inland Revenue—cross-checking in National Insurance records means that cases where an individual is receiving benefit while at the same time paying National Insurance contributions will tend to be discovered. Much economic activity associated with benefit fraud will thus overlap with economic activity concealed from the Inland Revenue. In trying to assess the overall scale of the black economy (that is, the amount of economic activity associated with tax evasion and benefit fraud) it may therefore be appropriate to concentrate on the scale of income tax evasion. That is not to say that the main motivation for the evasion will necessarily have been the objective of evading income tax, since for many benefit claimants the tax involved may be small. Indeed, where benefit fraud and tax evasion are combined, the motivation for the evasion may be complex, and may involve factors relating to each of the taxes and benefits concerned.

One consequence of this is that it will be difficult to translate an estimate of the amount of economic activity in the black economy into an estimate of the amounts of tax lost through evasion and of benefit lost through fraud. Tax evasion and benefit fraud involving misrepresentation of family circumstances, for example, will involve tax loss, without any corresponding hidden economic activity. Cases where income tax evasion is accompanied by either benefit fraud or the evasion of another tax, such as value added tax, will involve a higher tax loss in relation to the level of concealed economic activity than cases of income tax evasion alone.

Furthermore, even if it were possible to translate the size of the black economy into an estimate of the amount of tax evasion involved, it does not of course follow that policies to tighten up on tax evasion would succeed in recovering the tax. As the debate between Feige and McGee (1982) and Peacock and Shaw (1982) illustrates, much depends on how people are assumed to respond to a more rigorous enforcement policy. If moonlighters decide they would rather have extra free time than pay tax, then tougher enforcement may yield little revenue, and would merely reduce the amount of goods and services produced.

Understanding why tax evasion and benefit fraud occur is a first step to assessing the possible scale of such evasion and fraud, and to considering whether it might be more effectively controlled. This chapter aims to outline the ways in which economic theory approaches the issues of tax evasion and benefit fraud. Despite the wide range of taxes and benefits that may be subject to evasion, there are sufficient similarities between the different cases for a common theoretical framework to be developed. This theory is then used to provide a structure for the remaining chapters in this part.

Theoretical analysis of tax evasion

There is an extensive literature on the economic theory of tax evasion. This has recently been the subject of a useful survey by Cowell (1985), and it is not necessary here to duplicate his comprehensive review of the literature. Instead, what is intended in this section is to draw out a number of themes from the literature in order to provide an organising framework for the review of the empirical evidence in subsequent chapters.

The theoretical literature has been concerned with two main questions. Firstly, it has tried to describe and analyse tax evasion behaviour within a systematic theoretical framework; in other words, to produce a theoretical analysis of the causes of tax evasion. The second question has been about policy. Drawing on the theoretical models of the causes of tax evasion, the literature has considered what the appropriate public policy response should be. How much tax evasion is it desirable to seek to prevent, and what are the most appropriate ways of attempting to combat evasion?

Many of the early theoretical analyses of tax evasion, such as Allingham and Sandmo (1972), Srinivasan (1973), Kolm (1973), and Singh (1973), developed a theory of tax evasion based on the more general theory of portfolio selection. As Cowell (1985) observes, most of the results obtained from these models bear considerable similarities to results in the portfolio selection literature on the effects of taxation and risk in wealth allocation models. Subsequent theoretical research has moved in two directions. One, followed by Sandmo (1981), has involved the integration of the theory of tax evasion with the theory of labour supply, examining optimal taxation policy in the presence of tax evasion. The second direction taken has entailed modelling in a more sophisticated fashion the process of detection and enforcement, as in Reinganum and Wilde (1984) and Greenberg (1984).

Despite their comparative simplicity, the initial models of tax evasion based on portfolio selection theory provide a useful starting point for empirical analysis. These models assume that the individual's decision about whether to try to evade tax is based on, or at least reflects, a rational, profit-maximising calculation. Tax evasion, under this assumption, has potential benefits and potential costs to the individual concerned.

In the simplest models, the individual's pre-tax income (in the case of analyses of income tax evasion) is taken as given. The principal benefit to the individual of successful evasion is the saving of tax that would otherwise have to be paid. The potential costs, however, against which the benefit has to be weighed, are the risk of being caught and the penalties, including the possibility of fines and a criminal record, that could follow. The taxpayer is assumed to weigh up the costs of evasion, in terms of the risks and penalties, against the saving of tax. The higher the potential benefits in relation to the costs and risks of detection, the more likely an individual will be to try to evade tax.

Models of this sort, although they are very simple in structure, do tend to suggest some factors that may influence the scale of tax evasion. On the one hand, tax evasion would tend to be encouraged by higher rates of tax, because the financial savings from evasion would be correspondingly greater. On the other hand, tax evasion would be discouraged more, the higher the risk of being caught and the greater the punishment meted out to those who get caught. Chapters 5 and 7 consider the possible role of tax rates and enforcement policy in determining the scale of tax evasion in the UK, and in particular consider the evidence for the view that either increases in taxation or lax enforcement policy may have contributed to rapid growth in the black economy in the UK in recent years.

Although they may provide some useful insights into tax evasion, the realism of simple portfolio selection models of tax evasion is limited. A number of the complexities of evasion decisions and of enforcement policy cannot be analysed adequately within this framework. Sandmo (1981) has discussed a model in which the total amount of economic activity may be affected by tax rates and the scope for evasion. In this model, taxation acts to reduce the amount of paid work that people are prepared to do—there is a disincentive effect on labour supply. The theory of optimal taxation has explored the optimal income tax rate when taxation has a disincentive effect on labour; Sandmo's paper extends this analysis to a situation where the possibility of tax evasion means that people can supply labour in one of two ways. They can either work in the formal economy and be taxed, or supply labour in the black economy, where they are not taxed but run the risk of being caught and fined. If people differ in the amount of work they are prepared to do at different wage rates, in their attitudes to risk, or in other respects, some may choose to work in the formal economy and others to work in the black economy. If those who choose to work in the black economy are those whose labour supply is highly elastic with respect to the wage rate, then some tax evasion may actually be beneficial from the point of view of overall economic efficiency. Failure to enforce the tax fully may produce efficiency gains, because it would mean that an elastic part of the supply of labour was being taxed at a low effective rate.

Sandmo observes that considerations like this may be a partial explanation of the actual behaviour of tax authorities, 'who often seem reluctant to enforce the tax law in areas where efficiency losses would be substantial and are easy to identify'. However true this may be as an observation of fact, the model clearly illustrates the complex issues that should be considered in formulating policy towards tax evasion. If enforcement policies have the effect of reducing productive activity, either because people choose not to work if they are taxed or because the demand for certain goods and services falls if they are taxed, then effective enforcement may (depending on the size of these effects) be undesirable from the overall economic point of view. More vigorous enforcement may raise little revenue, but may reduce economic activity sharply.

From the point of view of enforcement policy, therefore, it would be necessary to identify the groups of the population who are most involved in tax evasion, and in each case to assess what effect a more vigorous enforcement policy would be likely to have on their labour supply and production decisions. It is certainly clear that there will be large differences between different groups of the population in the opportunities open to them to evade tax. As Chapter 6 shows, some people may find that their work or their social life brings them into contact with opportunities for casual work that can be concealed from the Inland Revenue. Others, such as the self-employed, may find that their work gives them more control over their tax affairs than the majority of the working population, whose income tax is deducted by their employers through the Pay-As-You-Earn (PAYE) system. Particular skills and occupations may be in demand in the black economy, and particular parts of the country may have higher levels of demand for black economy goods and services than others. Considerable variations would therefore be expected in the levels of tax evasion by different sections of the population, reflecting differences in the opportunities open to them. These differences in opportunity may also be accompanied by differences in the responsiveness of labour supply to taxation and tax enforcement—and hence, perhaps, may imply differences in the appropriate level of enforcement in different areas of evasion.

A second area where greater attempts at sophistication have been made is in the modelling of enforcement policy. In the simple models the risk of being caught evading tax is modelled as an externally given probability. Someone trying to evade tax will either be detected (and punished) or escape detection; the probability of detection does not depend on anything the taxpayer does. As Reinganum and Wilde (1984) have described, tax evasion differs from crimes such as burglary in that it involves making a report—in the form of a tax return—to the authorities. The possibility of influencing the risk of investigation and detection through the information disclosed in the tax return is quite real. As Chapter 7 describes, the Inland Revenue only investigates income tax payers when it has grounds for suspicion; successful tax evaders may organise their affairs so as to minimise the grounds for suspicion. This may often involve declaring a 'plausible' income level, so as to reduce the risk of investigation. In turn, behaviour of this sort would impose a natural limit on the extent of tax evasion, since even taxpayers with the opportunity to evade all taxes might nonetheless choose to declare a proportion of their income to avoid attracting the attention of the Revenue.

Another extension of the representation of enforcement policy has been in the analysis of the government's enforcement objectives. A straightforward assumption is that the government seeks to maximise its revenue from a given set of tax rates, after taking into account the costs of enforcement. However, this approach has limitations. In particular, consideration of the optimal balance between greater enforcement effort and higher penalties within this framework can lead to some startling results.

If the objective of the government is simply to maximise the revenue obtained from the tax system, then the least costly way of doing this will generally be to rely on extremely high penalties, while devoting negligible resources to detection. This is because a given level of deterrence can be obtained either by raising penalties (which has negligible costs in terms of resources) or by increasing the probability of detection (which may be extremely costly). So long as the objective of public policy is simply to maximise net revenues (gross tax revenues net of enforcement costs), then the role for detection in enforcement policy will be minimal.

As Sandmo (1981) has argued, the analysis may need to be extended by notions of risk aversion and equity or 'fairness' if the balance between penalty levels and investigation work in existing enforcement policies is to be properly understood. More generally, of course, a wider role for moral notions might be introduced into the analysis of tax evasion. The rational calculation of costs and benefits may be only one of the elements that will enter into a decision by any particular individual to evade tax. The moral attitude of the individual towards tax evasion may also be important, as well as the moral attitudes of other family members, social pressures, the psychological ability to rationalise or 'excuse' personal acts of law-breaking, and so on.

Summary

Economists have frequently analysed tax evasion using a model of rational decision-making. People are assumed to weigh up the personal benefits and costs of tax evasion, in terms of the saving of tax on the one hand, and the risk of detection and the scale of possible punishment on the other. The extent of tax evasion will be influenced by these variables, but in addition both the level and pattern of tax evasion will reflect the opportunities for evasion open to taxpayers in different occupations and circumstances.

The following three chapters examine factors that may have affected the level of tax evasion in the UK: Chapter 5 looks at the incentives that may have been generated by UK tax rates; Chapter 6 examines the opportunities for evasion open to different groups of the population; and Chapter 7 considers how enforcement policies may have contributed to the disincentives to evasion. Chapter 8 then considers how a similar complex of influences may have affected the level and pattern of benefit fraud in the UK.

Chapter 5

The incentives: tax rates

High tax rates on income and expenditure have been held to be one of the causes of the phenomenal growth in the black economy that some writers believe they have observed. High rates of income tax increase the gain to be made from concealing a part of earnings from the revenue authorities, while high rates of indirect taxation on expenditure (value added tax—VAT—in the UK) both increase the profits that can be made from seeking payment 'in cash', and increase the scope for 'honest' firms to be undercut by 'cowboys' who evade VAT.

Direct taxes

Generally, the aspect of the income tax structure that gives most cause for concern in the context of tax evasion is the marginal rate of income tax; that is, the extra income tax paid for each extra pound of income earned. The marginal rate is a measure of the tax that can be saved by concealing a part of total earnings while continuing to pay tax on the remainder. Most tax evasion is likely to be of this form: people with undeclared second jobs (moonlighters) will evade tax on their second-job earnings but continue to pay tax on their main earnings; and people who are in full-time self-employment will generally have more chance of evading tax on part of their income than of evading the Revenue's clutches altogether.

The average rate of income tax (i.e. total income tax paid as a percentage of earnings) is of less relevance to tax evasion, except for people who are able to evade the income tax system entirely. Such people, called 'ghosts' in Inland Revenue parlance, are probably few, and are likely to be concentrated in certain groups of the population—pensioners, illegal immigrants—who either have no need to maintain an adequate National Insurance record or have an overriding need to remain hidden. For 'ghosts' in the latter group, considerations other than the saving of tax are the main factors in their decision to conceal their employment, and it is unlikely that average tax rates will have much effect on their choice.

Marginal income tax rates in the UK depend on 'taxable income'; that is, the level of annual income after deducting the taxpayer's 'personal allowance'. This allowance, which is the level of income that can be received free of tax, is currently (1984/5) £3,155 for a married man and £2,055 for a single person. Few people in full-time employment have incomes below this level, and so nearly all people in full-time employment are subject to income tax at some level. The vast majority of taxpayers pay tax at the basic rate, currently 30 per cent, which is levied on the first £15,400 of taxable income. Only about 4 per cent of UK taxpayers pay income tax at higher marginal rates; the highest marginal rate—60 per cent—is levied on taxable income above £38,100 a year.

The basic rate of income tax has been broadly stable at between 30 and 35 per cent over the past three decades (Table 5.1). However, there has been a marked growth in the number of income tax payers, from less than four million immediately before the Second World War, to fourteen-and-a-half million in 1948/9, and over twenty million from the mid-1960s onwards (Table 5.2). It is the growth in the number of people caught by the income tax net, rather than in the rates of income tax levied, that is probably the more important change in the incentives to income tax evasion over the post-war period.

TABLE 5.1
Basic Rate of Income Tax

	Per cent
1955/6–1958/9	33.1
1959/60–1964/5	30.1
1965/6–1970/1	32.1
1971/2–1972/3	30.1
1973/4	30
1974/5	33
1975/6–1976/7	35
1977/8	34
1978/9	33
1979/80–1984/5	30

TABLE 5.2

Number of Taxpayers

	Number of taxpayers[a] (millions)	Percentage paying higher rates (surtax until 1973)
1938/9	3.8	2.8
1948/9	14.5	1.5
1958/9	17.7	2.2
1968/9	20.7	2.3
1973/4	19.7	2.0
1978/9	21.4	3.6
1983/4	20.5	3.7

[a] Treating married couples as one taxpayer.

Source: *Inland Revenue Statistics 1984*, Table 1.3.

The highest rate of income tax has undergone more significant changes than the basic rate in recent years. The highest marginal rate of combined income tax and surtax (a graduated supplement to income tax on higher incomes) was 18s6d in the pound (92.5 per cent) until 1959, compared with a top rate of tax on earned income of 83 per cent in the mid-1970s, and the top rate of 60 per cent in force since 1979. Comparisons of this sort are complicated by the existence of an investment income surcharge of up to 15 per cent on top of these rates, which was applied to investment income between 1973 and 1983. Taking this into account, the marginal rate of income tax for the highest-rate taxpayers was 98 per cent in the mid-1970s. In any event, while the rates of tax on higher incomes have received particular attention, their relevance to the growth of the black economy can easily be overstated. As Table 5.2 shows, the percentage of taxpayers subject to rates of income tax above the basic rate has not exceeded 4 per cent at any time; the percentage of taxpayers subject to the top rate of income tax has been even smaller—less than 1 per cent.

In addition to income tax, labour income in the UK is also subject to National Insurance (NI) contributions; and a similar payroll-based NI contribution is levied from employers. Between 1948 and 1961 both employee and employer NI contributions were flat-rate amounts, but an earnings-related element was then added, and in 1975 all the main NI contributions became earnings-related.

In 1978, the State Earnings-Related Pension Scheme was introduced, allowing employers to contract out, thus reducing both employee and employer contribution rates, in return for taking on some of the burden of pension payments. In 1983/4 revenues from NI contributions totaled £23.1 billion, compared with £33.2 billion collected from income tax.

The steady move over the past three decades towards an income-related system of NI contributions has had the effect of increasing sharply the overall direct marginal tax rate (income tax plus NI contributions) on earned incomes. As Figure 5.1 shows, the marginal rate of tax, including employee NI contributions, is at present 39 per cent over most of the range of income subject to basic rate income tax. Income above £13,000 is not subject to NI contributions, so there is a band of incomes, between £13,000 and the higher rate bands of income tax, over which the marginal overall direct tax rate falls to the basic 30 per cent rate of income tax.

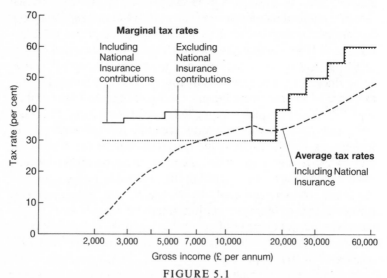

FIGURE 5.1

Average and Marginal Rates of Tax in the UK

Some forms of tax evasion may also involve evasion of employer NI contributions, as well as employee NI contributions and income tax. At present, employers who are not contracted out pay NI contributions at a rate of 11.45 per cent. The overall rate of combined tax and NI contributions is thus about 45 per cent (of incomes including employer NI contributions), implying a rise in the marginal overall tax rate on most employment incomes of about 50 per cent since 1960, with most of the rise being concentrated in the past ten years.

It has been noted (e.g. by Dilnot, Kay, and Morris, 1984b) that the basic rate of income tax exaggerates, by about six percentage points, the effective marginal rate of income tax relevant to labour supply decisions, since taxable income in the UK is computed after deductions whose incidence appears to be related to income. The most important of these deductions in recent years have been reliefs on mortgage interest, pension fund contributions, and life insurance premiums. Since people who earn more tend to spend more on these items, and hence to obtain higher deduction against tax, the effective marginal rate on additional earnings is overstated by the basic marginal rate. However, in considering whether to declare existing earnings or to try to evade tax on some part of existing earnings, such offsets work in the opposite direction. The choice for many potential tax evaders is not so much whether to earn more, as how much to declare. Disposable income, for people making this choice, will be higher if tax is evaded, and hence the benefit of income-related reliefs will be higher if tax is evaded. To the extent that this higher income allows higher expenditure on items that can be set against tax payments, the benefits from evading tax will be higher than indicated simply by the basic tax rate. Therefore the overall effect on evasion incentives of income-related reliefs is to magnify the effects of high rates of income tax (perhaps by an amount equivalent to two or three percentage points on the rate), rather than, as in the labour supply decision, to reduce the effects.

Indirect taxes

The most important indirect tax in the UK, and probably the most significant from the point of view of the black economy, is value added tax (VAT), which replaced the earlier system of purchase tax in 1973. The other indirect taxes, in particular the excise duties on petrol and oil, alcoholic drink, and tobacco, are especially tightly

STAFFORDSHIRE
POLYTECHNIC
LIBRARY

controlled, and despite very high tax rates are probably subject to little evasion.

Purchase tax had been introduced during the war as a tax on the wholesale value of a fairly wide range of goods, excluding those already subject to excise duties (e.g. drink and tobacco), services, and most 'essential' items such as food. Purchase tax was charged at up to seven different rates at any one time, and there were frequent changes in the rates.

VAT, by contrast, is levied on the value added at each stage of production of a wide range of both goods and services. It was introduced at a uniform rate of 10 per cent, but for five years between 1974 and 1979 was levied at a basic rate of 8 per cent and a luxury rate of 12.5 per cent. Since 1979 the rate of VAT has been 15 per cent.

For goods previously subject to purchase tax, the changes in the tax rates following the introduction of VAT may have had some marginal effect on the incentives to conduct business in the black economy. However, from the point of view of the incentives to evade tax, the most significant changes in indirect taxation have been in the point at which the tax is levied, and in the range of goods and services subject to tax.

The move from purchase tax, levied on wholesalers, to VAT, levied at all stages of the production and distribution chain, increased the number of individuals and companies paying tax from 74,000 to over one million. This is despite the fact that, in order to keep the number of tax points within bounds, very small companies (currently those with a turnover of less than £18,000) are not subject to the tax. The increase in the number of companies on whom indirect taxes are levied has both increased the number of potential tax evaders and made the job of enforcement harder.

Since VAT is levied on services as well as goods, the replacement of purchase tax by VAT brought the products of a large number of companies into the indirect tax net for the first time. Many services, especially those (such as painting, decorating, and house repairs) supplied by small firms to private households, seem—at least on the evidence of anecdotes—to be particularly prone to evasion. The size of the black economy may well have been increased by the extension of indirect taxes to cover services as well as goods.

Other taxes

The foregoing are the main sources of central government tax revenue in the UK. Other taxes that could in principle be evaded include corporation tax and other taxes on business and capital, domestic rates, and vehicle excise duty. To keep this study within manageable bounds, we have not considered in detail the incentives and opportunities for evasion presented by any of these taxes. This reflects both our judgement that public concern is greatest about evasion of the taxes we have chosen to cover, and our belief that the extent to which evasion of these other taxes may lead to underestimation of national income or gross domestic product is comparatively slight.

Summary

There are three principal respects in which the tax system in the UK has changed in the post-war period so as to increase the incentives for tax evasion. Firstly, the number of taxpayers subject to income tax rose sharply in the first decade or so after the war, although it has remained broadly constant since the mid-1960s. Secondly, while income tax rates, especially the rates faced by the bulk of taxpayers, have been quite stable, the marginal rate of taxation on income overall has risen, due to the introduction of earnings-related National Insurance contributions in 1961. Thirdly, the introduction of value added tax to replace purchase tax in 1973 involved a dramatic increase in the number of companies and individuals paying tax. For the first time, many service industries became subject to taxation.

Chapter 6

Opportunities for tax evasion

Due to the Pay-As-You-Earn (PAYE) system of income tax collection, evasion of income tax by employees on earnings from their main job is likely to be negligible. Greater scope for income tax evasion exists for the self-employed, who are not covered by the PAYE system, and on earnings from second jobs and casual income.

Operation of PAYE

Under the PAYE system income tax is deducted at source by the employer from employees' wages and salaries. A new employee's National Insurance (NI) number is communicated to the Inland Revenue, which is able to trace his or her tax office and individual tax records. The employer is then notified of the employee's tax code, which (in conjuction with a book of tables supplied by the Inland Revenue) allows the employer to withhold appropriate amounts for tax and NI contributions from the employee's weekly or monthly pay. The records of how this has been done have to be kept in a particular standard format, including carbon copies of pay-slips issued to employees, to facilitate monitoring by the Inland Revenue.

Evasion of income tax and NI contributions collected through PAYE could in principle take one of two forms. False accounting by the employer without the knowledge or involvement of employees would be one possibility. However, the scope for misrepresenting wages paid and tax deducted without the connivance of the employees involved is severely restricted by the independent check that the Inland Revenue gets from employees' own tax returns. For this reason it is likely that straightforward false accounting of wages and PAYE deductions by employers is likely to be very rare, and few cases will remain undetected for long.

More substantial scope for evasion within PAYE can exist if the employee is prepared to be a party to the evasion. This will normally require that the proceeds of the fraud are shared with colluding employees, but since the marginal rate of tax (including NI deductions) on most incomes is at least 40 per cent, there would still appear to be considerable mutual financial benefit to both employer and employee from income tax evasion. Nevertheless, there are some major disadvantages to such arrangements which may offset these financial benefits. Firstly, while the employer may have 'saved' some proportion of income tax by under-reporting his wages bill, this will have had the effect of substantially overstating the trading profit made (since in the assessment of trading profit, wage costs will now be understated). This illusory increase in profits will normally be taxed, reducing the overall gain to the employer. To avoid this offset, employers would need to achieve a more comprehensive deception of the tax authorities, involving 'off-the-books' revenue items as well.

Such a move has considerable ramifications for the organisation and internal accounting systems of the firm. These are discussed in some detail below in relation to evasion of value added tax (VAT), and it is concluded that they may involve a risk of a substantial loss of internal control and efficiency, except in very small firms, where the owner is able to exert close personal control over management and accounting.

Collusive action by employer and employees to evade income tax will also affect the balance of power between them, possibly with unpredictable effects. Generally, in day-to-day matters the effect will often be to worsen the position of employees, particularly in matters like access to unfair dismissals procedure and other forms of legal protection from exploitation. But the employer, too, is vulnerable—to the actions of a disgruntled employee, who can inform the Inland Revenue of what is going on. The instability introduced by these changes in the power relationships within the firm make it unlikely that wise owners or managers will seek to make collusive deals with their employees over PAYE, or that many such deals (especially in larger firms with less 'personal' management) would last all that long.

The self-employed are in a different position in that they have control over the reporting of their own income to the Inland Revenue. Also, self-employed people are not taxed through the PAYE system; instead, tax is both assessed and paid in arrears.

There is undoubtedly greater scope for concealment when dealing with one's own tax affairs, and the self-employed are also able to offset a much wider range of expenses against income than can people taxed as employees. Overstating allowable expenses, rather than plain under-reporting of income, may be a second source of tax underpayment.

Tax evasion and the self-employed

About one in ten of the UK working population is self-employed. Self-employment is heavily concentrated in particular industries: in agriculture, where about two-fifths of the workforce are self-employed; in construction, where over a quarter are self-employed; and in distribution, hotels and catering, and repair businesses, where the proportion self-employed is about one in seven. By contrast, less than 3 per cent of the workforce of manufacturing industry is self-employed. (Table 6.1.)

During the 1950s and 1960s the percentage of the working population who were self-employed remained broadly constant. However, total self-employment incomes fell from about $14\frac{1}{2}$ per cent of total income from employment and self-employment in 1951 to less than 12 per cent in 1971. This decline in the income share of the self-employed could, of course, reflect a genuine relative improvement in the earning position of employees; equally, it might reflect increasing tax evasion in self-employment incomes.

Most self-employed people will report a proportion of their income, so as to avoid arousing the suspicion of the Inland Revenue. This puts an upper limit on the amount of income on which it is plausible that tax could be evaded. However, it is likely that the self-employed nevertheless have considerable scope for tax evasion. In 1976, Tony Christopher, General Secretary of the Inland Revenue Staff Federation, commented that the low incomes actually declared by the self-employed 'defy belief'. At that time only 70,000 (out of a total self-employed population of nearly two million) declared earnings equal to or greater than the average wage (then about £60), and only one in eight owned up to an income of more than £30 a week. Whilst there are, of course, good reasons for some self-employed people having low earnings (e.g. because they only work part-time, or because they are just starting up in business, or because their business shows little profit) it seems clear

TABLE 6.1

Self-Employed People: Industrial Analysis,
June figures in thousands (figures in parentheses are as percentage of total employment)

Division	Great Britain	1971	1973	1975	1977	1979	1981	1983
0–9	All industries and services	1,954	1,969	1,933	1,843	1,842	2,057	2,199
	%	(8.3)	(8.2)	(8.0)	(7.7)	(7.5)	(8.8)	(9.7)
0	Agriculture, forestry, fishing	282	259	247	254	257	250	246
	%	(40.1)	(38.1)	(38.9)	(40.2)	(41.7)	(42.2)	(42.1)
2–4	Manufacturing industry	129	133	140	142	140	146	154
	%	(1.6)	(1.7)	(1.9)	(1.9)	(1.9)	(2.3)	(2.7)
5	Construction	342	439	362	291	343	388	413
	%	(22.7)	(25.6)	(22.9)	(19.8)	(22.0)	(25.9)	(29.5)
6–9	Service industries	1,200	1,138	1,183	1,155	1,102	1,273	1,386
	%	(9.6)	(8.6)	(8.6)	(8.3)	(7.7)	(8.8)	(9.6)
6	Distribution, hotels, catering, repairs	726	677	680	678	636	698	716
	%	(16.8)	(14.9)	(14.8)	(14.6)	(13.2)	(14.6)	(14.9)
7	Transport and communication	65	70	78	80	87	99	94
	%	(4.1)	(4.5)	(5.0)	(5.3)	(5.7)	(6.6)	(6.7)
8	Banking, finance, insurance, etc.	148	144	157	148	145	188	220
	%	(10.1)	(9.2)	(9.7)	(9.0)	(8.1)	(9.9)	(10.9)
9	Other services	261	247	268	249	234	288	356
	%	(5.0)	(4.5)	(4.5)	(4.1)	(3.8)	(4.6)	(5.7)

Sources: *Employment Gazette,* July 1984, p. 321 (self-employment estimates).
Employment Gazette Historical Supplement no. 1, April 1985, p. 8 (employees in employment).

that understatement by the self-employed must be wide-spread, and the task of the Inland Revenue in controlling evasion must be substantial.

As we have already seen (in Chapter 3), the Central Statistical Office (CSO)'s estimates of national income do make substantial allowance for incomes from self-employment not reported to the Inland Revenue. This estimated component, which is based in part on the views of the Inland Revenue about unreported self-employment income, amounted to some one-seventh of total self-employment income in 1980–2. A similar percentage would be consistent with the discrepancies between incomes and expenditures of employees and the self-employed reported to the Family Expenditure Survey (see Chapter 12).

The prolonged recession since 1979 seems to have been accompanied by a sharp rise in the number of people self-employed in Britain. Overall, the number of self-employed was 19 per cent higher in 1983 than in 1979, and the percentage of the employed workforce who were self-employed rose even more sharply, from 7.5 per cent of the total in 1979 to 9.5 per cent in 1983. The percentage self-employed has risen in all the industry groups shown in Table 6.1, but especially in the construction industry.

It is difficult yet to disentangle the factors that lie behind the recent revival of self-employment. Incentives on the 'supply side' could account for some part of the rise—for example, redundant workers setting up in business on their own account. Another factor may have been the development of a climate in which 'enterprise' is encouraged, and the tax and administrative burdens on small business lessened. In addition, some part of the growth in self-employment may reflect changes in either technology or management practice, leading to the subcontracting of certain services formerly performed 'in house'. Subcontracting of specialist services permits greater flexibility in their use, and reduces overheads. There seems to be an increasing tendency to subcontract activities such as computer services, marketing and public relations, and even design and tool-room functions in some engineering companies. One indicator of this trend has been the significant rise in self-employment in business services during the 1980s, from 156,000 in 1981 to 189,000 in 1983.

The implications for tax evasion and for the scale of uncounted output differ depending on which explanation is considered.

Enterprises set up by the unemployed will generally tend to have low net incomes—at least initially—and the evidence is that many fail within a year or so. Even if a large percentage of the net income from such businesses is undeclared, the tax loss may be small. The 'hiving off' of specialist services may pose a more serious problem, since the net income of the business will be higher. On the other hand, most such businesses will need to be integrated into the VAT system (since their main customers will be companies—rather than private individuals—which will want to be able to reclaim VAT on purchases, and to provide evidence of purchases). This will tend to mean that at least some of the turn-over of businesses supplying business services as subcontractors will have to be conducted 'on-the-books' and the scope for evasion will tend to be restricted if the suspicions of the Inland Revenue and VAT inspectors are not to be aroused.

Self-employment in construction

The recent sharp rise in self-employment in the construction industry shown in Table 6.1 must be a matter for some concern to the Inland Revenue. Tax evasion in the construction industry is popularly regarded as wide-spread, not only because of the scope for moonlighting, but also because of the growth of labour-only subcontracting (LOSC), known colloquially as the 'lump'. LOSC differs from the more conventional form of subcontracting—'supply and fix'—in that the subcontractor does not supply any materials but only supplies labour services. Payment is usually on a piece-work basis. The Phelps Brown Committee, which reported on labour-only subcontracting in the late 1960s—by which time the rapid growth of this practice had become a matter of some public concern—noted that one factor in the growth of LOSC was that it allowed workers to avoid the PAYE system by becoming self-employed subcontractors. Since income tax is collected through PAYE on a current basis but assessed and collected from the self-employed in arrears, moving from employee to self-employed status makes it possible to defer payments by some eighteen months. In addition, the scope for evasion by under-reporting income may be considerably greater. (Not all labour-only subcontractors were found to be self-employed individuals, though probably more than half were. A number of firms undertook labour-only subcontracting too.)

But the Phelps Brown Committee also noted the benefits of the practice, in improving the flexibility and efficiency in employment of specialist workers. A survey in 1967 by the National Federation of Building Trades Employers of labour-only subcontracting in private house-building found that it was most frequent in skilled occupations such as bricklaying, carpentry and joinery, and plastering, where it gave the employer the ability to employ such specialist workers only when actually needed on-site. LOSC payments averaged about a quarter of the payments for labour on the average site, and the Committee estimated that about two-thirds of those self-employed in the construction industry were engaged on labour-only subcontracting.

To control the extent of tax evasion through labour-only subcontracting in the building industry, a special tax-deduction scheme for the industry was introduced in 1971. This required firms employing labour-only subcontractors to make a deduction on behalf of the Inland Revenue of about 30 per cent from the payments made for subcontracting. Subcontractors could, however, be exempted from this arrangement if they were in possession of an exemption certificate. These certificates were to be awarded only to established subcontractors who could demonstrate a good record of paying tax. Due to wide-spread malpractice, including the forgery and sale of exemption certificates, the procedures were tightened in 1975 after which they were widely regarded as having almost completely closed the loophole provided by the 'lump'. A considerable level of self-employment in the construction industry remained, including considerable labour-only subcontracting (reflecting the flexibility and other non-fiscal advantages of LOSC arrangements), but the sharp drop in the numbers of self-employed in the construction industry in the mid-1970s may well reflect the introduction of the tax-deduction scheme.

Lobbying by the construction industry has led to a relaxation of the provisions of the tax-deduction scheme since 1980, and anecdotal evidence suggests that the recession has encouraged a considerably greater number of construction firms to turn to LOSC as a way of cutting costs and improving flexibility. The 40 per cent rise in self-employment in the construction industry since 1977 may well have taken place for reasons that have nothing to do with tax evasion, but there is no doubt that it has substantially increased the number of people in a position to evade tax, in an industry with a long history of tax enforcement problems. Nevertheless, the use of the deduction scheme has probably placed bounds on the tax lost through subcontracting, and in general it can be said that the scope for tax evasion by labour-only subcontractors is likely to be less than the scope afforded to other self-employed people.

Second jobs and tax evasion

Another group who would appear to have some scope for income tax evasion are second-job holders. About one-third of second jobs are held in a self-employed capacity (General Household Survey, 1981, p. 85). In addition, second-job earnings from employment will often be sufficiently low to fall below the PAYE threshold (currently £38.50 per week), and will therefore not be taxed automatically at source. While the Inland Revenue nonetheless obtains from employers details of the names, addresses, and wages paid to employees earning below the PAYE threshold and do try to match this information to the subsequent tax returns of the employees involved, this procedure is clearly less infallible than PAYE deduction at source, and greater scope for evasion exists.

Second-job holding in the UK has been studied by Alden (1981) and Brown, Levin, Rosa, and Ulph (1984), using information from a variety of statistical sources. There were considerable differences in the rates of double-job holding found in different surveys. Alden reported that the Family Expenditure Survey (FES) identified 7.3 per cent of the labour force holding two jobs in 1976, while the General Household Survey (GHS) put the figure at 3 per cent. Brown *et al.* reported even more variation between different estimates, with second-job activity rates varying from 3 per cent to 12 per cent (Table 6.2).

Part of the variation in the rates of second-job holding in the different surveys seems to be due to the time-horizon used in the survey question asked. The GHS asked whether a second job had been held in the previous week, while the FES asked about second jobs without a specific time-frame. The Treasury survey reported by Brown *et al.* asked about second-job activity 'in the last month' and yielded an answer roughly intermediate between the GHS ('last

TABLE 6.2

Percentage of Main-Job Holders Also Having a Second Job

Survey (Time-frame)	1971	1980
GHS (1 week)	3.1%	3.5%
Treasury (1 month)		5.2%
FES (no time-frame)	6.9%	8.3%
SSRC (no time-frame)	11.8%	

Source: Brown, Levin, Rosa, and Ulph, 1984, pp. 5–6.

week') and the FES (no time-frame specified). The implication of this—that a high percentage of second jobs are held only intermittently—is given further support by the results of additional questions in the 1981 GHS, which aimed to quantify the effects of different time-frames on the rates of second-job holding. Whilst only 4 per cent of job holders in the 1981 GHS reported having had a second job 'last week', a total of 7 per cent of job holders reported that they had a second job when no time-frame was specified.

The high rate of second-job holding discovered by the 1971 Social Science Research Council (SSRC) survey cannot, however, be explained simply in terms of the indefinite time-frame employed, since the rate is much higher than the comparable rate identified by the 1971 FES, which also specified no time-horizon in the question. Brown *et al.* (1984) observe that another possible source of difference may have been in the reactions of respondents to the questions asked. The SSRC study adopted a 'funnel' approach by first introducing the topic of extra work in a very general and non-threatening way before asking for details. It succeeded in getting a much higher percentage response to the initial general question (about whether people 'do extra work in their spare time'—to which 15 per cent replied that they did) than to later questions such as 'How much does that bring in a week?' and 'Are there any deductions?'. Only 7.2 per cent answered this final question, and of them only about a quarter said there would be deductions. Clearly some percentage of second-job holders are cautious about going into much detail about their second jobs in surveys, and this fact must indicate caution in interpreting FES data on second-job holding, both about its level (since in 1971 this appeared to be understated in relation to the SSRC survey) and about its pattern (since tax evasion on second jobs may not be random, but may be facilitated by the characteristics of either the jobs or their holders).

Second jobs are most likely to be held by people unable to vary the total hours worked in their main job. Where people have the opportunity of working overtime in their main job, it is plausible to suppose that some will choose to earn extra income in this way rather than by taking a second job, especially since overtime rates may well be particularly advantageous in relation to the possible hourly earnings from casual employment. It is likely that any reduction in the availability of overtime will have increased the number of people seeking second jobs. Similarly, the reduction in working hours and the spread of 'flexitime' are likely to have increased second-job holding.

It does not, however, appear that there is any straightforward association between the number of hours people work in their main job and the percentage of people holding second jobs. Table 6.3, based on analysis of Family Expenditure Survey data for 1982, shows that the percentage of men holding second jobs tends, if anything, to rise as the number of hours worked in the main job rises. Female second-job holders, however, tend to be more common amongst those working fewer hours in their main job.

TABLE 6.3

Hours Worked and Second-Job Holding

Hours worked in main job	Percentage of people holding two jobs	
	Men	Women
Under 30	4.8	5.5
30–35	4.3	3.4
35–40	5.1	3.4
40–45	4.5	2.8
45–50	5.9	...[a]
Over 50	3.8	...[a]

[a] Insufficient observations.

Source: Analysis of a sample of 4,200 households included in the 1982 Family Expenditure Survey.

Table 6.4 shows an analysis of second-job holding by occupation. A lot of second-job holding is by professional workers in public administration and business—people whose main jobs perhaps afford little scope for flexibility in the hours worked and who have skills they may be able to make use of in second jobs. By contrast, people in occupations where overtime is often available (e.g. manufacturing) or where the hours they work in their main job can be varied if desired (e.g. self-employed workers in construction) are less likely to have second jobs.

The kinds of occupations held as second jobs can also be seen from Table 6.4. Overall, the GHS found that only about one-third of second jobs were in the same kind of occupation as the person's main job. Few second jobs are in manufacturing and repairing occupations, which account for about one-third of main jobs. On the other hand, some occupations account for a much larger proportion of second jobs than of main jobs: about 10 per cent of second jobs held by men are in security occupations, about one-fifth of womens' second jobs involve selling, and over two-fifths are in catering, cleaning, hairdressing, and other personal services.

Two broad categories of second-job holding may be suggested. One involves the application of main-job skills in a second area. An accountant employed by a local authority might, for example, take on a part-time second job working for a private company. Second jobs of this sort will generally involve high skill levels and correspondingly high earnings. Capital requirements, however, will generally have to be low, particularly if the job is held in a self-employed capacity, if part-time work is to be profitable in competition with full-time competitors. (The exception would be if the capital equipment can be 'borrowed' from the main job.) Some part-time jobs of this sort may be undertaken with the ultimate objective of developing a full-time business, and part-time work may provide a way of 'testing the water' before setting up in business on one's own.

The second group of second jobs are those held in a completely different area from the main job. Usually they will involve much lower skill levels, both in relation to the first group and in relation to skill levels in the main job. Examples would be such generally poorly paid activities as bar-work and cleaning. Second jobs of this sort may have been hit quite hard in recent years by competition from the unemployed.

TABLE 6.4

Second-Job Holding by Occupation Group

Occupation group	MEN			WOMEN		
	Occupation group of main jobs (%)	Occupation group of second jobs (%)	Percentage of main-job holders with second jobs (%)	Occupation group of main jobs (%)	Occupation group of second jobs (%)	Percentage of main-job holders with second jobs (%)
Professional and related supporting management in education, welfare, and health	5	15	10	13	14	5
Literary, artistic, and sports	1	12	11	1	3	1
Other professional and managerial	24	24	3	7	6	3
Clerical and related	7	5	4	32	12	4
Selling	4	4	4	10	19	2
Security and protective service	2	10	2	0	0	1
Catering, cleaning, hairdressing, and other personal services	4	11	3	23	43	4
Farming, fishing, and related	2	5	4	1	1	5
Manufacturing, repairing, etc.	32	6	2	13	1	2
Construction, mining	6	2	2	0	0	0
Other	12	8	3	1	0	4
Total/All occupations	100	100	3	100	100	4

Source: General Household Survey, 1981.

The incentives to declare income from second jobs may be complex. People holding two jobs may be reluctant to let their principal employer know about their second job. Some employers, for example, may believe that second jobs adversely affect work effort or motivation in the first job, or reduce availability for overtime if required. Since the PAYE coding supplied by the Inland Revenue to the first employer will usually reflect second-job earnings (although special arrangements can be implemented to prevent this), information about the existence of the second job will be communicated indirectly to the main employer if second-job earnings are declared.

On the other hand, the main employer may approve even less if his employee is discovered to be evading income tax, and professional associations too may take a dim view of criminal proceedings for tax evasion. This may limit the extent to which earnings from such second jobs are simply not declared, but other, possibly less 'risky', ways of reducing tax liability—perhaps through barter of services or overstating expenses—may be more common.

Even if many people holding second jobs do not declare their earnings from such jobs for tax, the tax losses are unlikely to be great in relation to the total income tax yield. Second jobs are held by only a proportion of the population, generally for only a few hours a week, and some may be quite poorly paid. Brown, Levin, Rosa, and Ulph (1984) estimate that total income earned in second jobs was only about 0.8 per cent of total income earned in main jobs. Even if tax were evaded on two-thirds of this income, the amount of tax lost from second-job tax evasion would amount to only about 1 per cent of Inland Revenue income tax receipts.

VAT evasion

Revenue lost through VAT evasion is likely to be a comparatively small percentage of total VAT revenue. As Kay and King (1983) pointedly remark, 'It is a fact that most economic activity in the UK is in the hands of large organizations which as a matter of course comply with legal requirements to report income and output and to withhold tax'.

There are good reasons that this should be so. Evading VAT on any significant scale would require keeping a second—or at the very least one fictitious—set of records and accounts. And this would inevitably involve making a number of the employees of the firm party to the deception. Not only does this put the firm at the mercy of a disaffected employee, but it also reduces managerial control over other frauds and losses that might go on. Once employees have been taught how their company can deceive Customs and Excise, employees may apply the same methods to deceive their employer. Control of the 'real business' rather than the fictitious one developed for the VAT inspectors' eyes will necessarily be poorly documented, and therefore will be weaker than in an 'honest' firm.

Another reason that large firms are unlikely to try to evade VAT is that the managers who need to implement the fraud frequently have no financial interest in the profitability of the firm. Much of the economic literature on managerial motivation argues that, in large firms, due to the separation of ownership and control, profit maximisation may be a relatively unimportant objective for managers. Managers in large firms may pursue other objectives, such as sales maximisation, instead; also, their behaviour often suggests that they are risk-averse. They are unlikely to try to evade tax to increase the wealth of shareholders, at considerable personal risk.

For these reasons we would expect VAT evasion to be practically nil except in small firms where the owner retains direct control over all aspects of the firm's activity and the relevant documentation. While such small companies are numerous, the smallest (at present those with turn-over less than £19,500 a year) are exempt from VAT, and in total they account for a relatively small percentage of output. Moreover, even for small firms there are forces acting to limit the extent to which they try to evade VAT.

Transactions in intermediate products—such as the sale of components by one firm to another—are subject to VAT, but the purchasing firm can claim back the VAT paid on the components and other inputs that it purchases. To the purchasing firm, therefore, there is little advantage in purchasing inputs from a firm evading VAT (although due to the infrequency of cross-checking between the records of purchase and sale in inter-firm transactions, there is scope for fraudulently reclaiming VAT on non-existent purchases). Similarly, companies with substantial inputs on which VAT has been paid will have an incentive to declare a large proportion of their output so as to have an adequate and plausible output level in relation to these inputs.

In conclusion, therefore, we would expect evasion of VAT to be confined in the main to those areas where it has been most widely talked about—*viz.* sales of generally labour-intensive goods and services to private households and consumers by self-employed workers or very small businesses. Many of the smallest businesses—and nearly all self-employed moonlighters—will in any case be exempt, and where they demand payment in cash this may simply reflect uncertainty and misinformation about the VAT system, or more likely reflect the evasion of other taxes, especially income tax. Nevertheless, large-scale VAT frauds are possible and have on occasion been detected; the possibility that more remain, undetected, cannot be ruled out.

Summary

This chapter has looked at two groups of people who may have a greater opportunity to evade income tax than the bulk of employees, whose income tax is deducted at source through PAYE. The self-employed have particular scope for evading tax, and their numbers have increased sharply since 1979. Substantial allowance is already included in the UK national accounts for incomes unreported by the self-employed, to the extent of about one-seventh of self-employment income in 1980–2. Second jobs also provide scope for income tax evasion, but the tax lost through such evasion is probably low, since total incomes earned in second jobs may be less than 1 per cent of income earned in main jobs.

The quantitative importance of VAT evasion is harder to assess. VAT evasion is most likely to be confined to the smallest firms, where the owner maintains direct managerial and financial control, and is more likely on sales of goods and services to private households than on those to other businesses.

Chapter 7

Tax evasion: detection, prosecution, and penalties

Responsibility for collecting and enforcing income tax and corporation tax in the UK rests with the Inland Revenue; value added tax (VAT) and excise duties are collected by HM Customs and Excise. The burden of collection of both VAT and income tax falls largely on businesses, which act as tax collectors not only for VAT but also under the Pay-As-You-Earn (PAYE) regulations. Employees who pay income tax through PAYE, who form the great majority of individual taxpayers, have by contrast little or no contact with either the Inland Revenue or Customs and Excise, and little experience of their enforcement powers.

These enforcement powers have evolved gradually over a considerable period; as the Keith Committee on the Enforcement Powers of the Revenue Departments, which reported in 1983, observed, 'they have grown up as an historical hotchpotch without any comprehensive scheme or logical framework'. The VAT enforcement powers of Customs and Excise are generally regarded as more comprehensive than those available to the Inland Revenue to enforce collection of income taxes. As with the purchase tax which VAT superseded, Customs and Excise has the power to enter business premises to make inspections and examine business records for the purpose of verifying the accuracy of returns. Such 'control' visits give Customs and Excise effective powers of random investigation for VAT evasion. The Inland Revenue's powers do not permit random investigation for evasion by individual taxpayers, and the powers available to verify suspect tax returns, although somewhat enhanced in the 1976 Finance Act, are less extensive than the powers of investigation given to Customs and Excise.

It is clearly impossible to make an accurate quantification of the risk of detection faced by someone attempting to evade VAT or income tax. The number of taxpayers who get away with tax evasion cannot be known; only those who are caught come to light. Whilst the balance of risks is thus difficult to assess, there are a number of indications, based on the resources devoted to investigation and their yield, that may make it possible to draw tentative inferences about the effectiveness of the enforcement efforts of the two Revenue departments.

Income tax enforcement

The investigation of tax evasion by the Inland Revenue falls under three broad headings: investigation by local offices, in-depth investigation of complex or specialised frauds by Enquiry Branch and other specialised units, and PAYE Audit. Local tax offices form the 'front line' of the department's anti-evasion effort, undertaking the vast majority of taxpayer investigations—about 70,000 cases settled in 1983/4 compared with about 1,000 by Enquiry Branch and Special Offices combined. Their investigations are begun only where there is reason to suspect tax evasion; by contrast, the PAYE Audit units, which check employers' operation of PAYE and the Special Deduction Scheme for the construction industry (described in Chapter 6), involve a degree of random control—although increasingly PAYE Audit visits too are being targeted on areas where irregularities are thought to be most likely.

The largest part of local tax office work is directed at the investigation of traders' accounts, including both the Schedule D income tax returns submitted by the self-employed and the tax returns of companies. Most accounts are accepted after only brief scrutiny (see Table 7.1), but local offices investigate about 3 per cent of Schedule D accounts in depth each year, and somewhat less than 1 per cent of company accounts.

The majority of these in-depth investigations yield some return: in 1981, 87 per cent of cases investigated resulted in some adjustment being made to profits—and hence additional tax charges (Keith Committee, Table 21). The yield from in-depth investigations settled at local offices in 1981 was £92 million, of which 70 per cent reflected additional tax and National Insurance contributions and 30 per cent reflected interest and other penalties (Keith Committee, Table 22). The average additional tax yield per case investigated appears to have been roughly £1,000 in

TABLE 7.1

Inland Revenue Treatment of Traders' Accounts 1980/1

	Schedule D accounts		Companies	
	(thous.)	(%)	(thous.)	(%)
Accepted after brief scrutiny	1,482	90.9	352	66.4
Reviewed for technical points	99	6.1	175	33.0
Examined in depth	49	3.0	3	0.6
Total	1,630	100	530	100

Source: Keith Committee Report, 1983, Table 19.

1981—which might suggest an average profit understatement of the order of £3,000 in the cases where an adjustment was made.

It is clear that when the Inland Revenue does investigate Schedule D and company accounts it finds a considerable level of tax evasion. This does not of course mean that on average all Schedule D and company accounts involve evasion to that extent, since tax offices presumably choose to investigate those where evasion is most blatant and those where the greatest amounts appear to be involved. On the other hand, the fact that only 3 per cent of Schedule D returns are investigated each year is a result of resource limitations. Not all cases where tax evasion is suspected may be investigated.

A random compliance study, based on investigation of a random sample of taxpayers, would be the best way of assessing how much tax evasion went undetected. Whilst the Inland Revenue does not have the power to undertake investigations at random, a pilot study undertaken in 1981 makes it possible to assess what proportion of suspect cases remain uninvestigated due to lack of resources (see Keith Committee, para.10.8.2). A random sample of 5,500 Schedule D tax returns by the self-employed was drawn, and District Inspectors were asked to categorise them, on the basis of their experience, as to whether they thought that an investigation, if started, would reveal an understatement of profit. One in five accounts involved, in the Inspectors' view, 'probable understatement' of income and a further two in every five 'possible understatement' of income. In four-fifths of the category involving probable understatement, the Inspectors judged that sufficient grounds for starting an investigation actually existed.

If 3 per cent of Schedule D accounts are investigated annually, the Inland Revenue reckons that over a five-year cycle a total of 12 per cent of accounts will be investigated, after allowing for businesses starting up and ceasing to trade and assuming that no case is investigated twice. Most of the 16 per cent of Schedule D accounts involving probable understatement and where investigation could be justified would thus appear likely to be covered over a five-year period—although only one in five of the total of cases involving probable and possible understatement of income would. The Keith Committee reported that a validation exercise was being undertaken on the pilot compliance study, to assess the extent of actual evasion, especially within the 'possible understatement' category.

Compared with the self-employed taxpayers taxed under Schedule D, employees and other 'non-trading' taxpayers have little contact with the Inland Revenue and have generally been the subject of comparatively little investigation work. The operation of the PAYE system, by which employers deduct employees' income tax at source, is monitored by PAYE Audit units. Compliance is generally believed to be good, and the cost:yield ratio of PAYE Audit at 1:4 is markedly lower than that of local tax offices (1:6) and Enquiry Branch, which investigates cases of serious fraud in business accounts (1:13).

Investigation of individual employee taxpayers is limited. Only one in three Schedule E taxpayers even receives an income tax form in any given year, and the onus is on individual taxpayers to declare any casual earnings. As the Keith Committee observed, this, together with the fact that the income tax form does not ask explicitly about casual earnings, may well be a contributory factor to the amount of moonlighting income not declared for tax.

A new departure, however, has been the growth in resources devoted to controlling aspects of the black economy such as moonlighting and the activities of 'ghost' workers, which had received little attention from the existing investigation work. The 1983 Inland Revenue Annual Report mentioned an experimental deployment of seventy staff in local offices to seek out 'moonlighters' and 'ghosts' which it said had proved 'cost effective' and 'very successful'. This experiment has been followed by the deployment of 850 additional staff on this work—the so-called 'ghostbusters'.

The penalties for tax evasion that is discovered by the Inland Revenue range from settlements for additional tax, through settlements for tax and interest or penalty charges, to prosecution. The overwhelming majority of Inland Revenue investigations result in settlements for tax (with or without interest and penalties added), and very few cases are brought before the Courts. Table 7.2 shows the pattern of prosecutions brought by the Inland Revenue in the past sixteen years. Most are for fraudulent use of the subcontractor exemption certificates used to administer the tax deduction scheme in the construction industry, or for the theft of payable orders and Giro cheques. Only about twenty-five prosecutions are made annually for false accounts or returns of

TABLE 7.2

Inland Revenue: Criminal Proceedings, annual averages

	Number of convictions			
	1968/9 –1971/2	1972/3 –1975/6	1976/7 1979/80	1980/1 –1983/4
False accounts or returns of income	16	14	25	25
False claims to personal allowances, deductions for expenses, and repayments	110	39	18	14
PAYE offences	14	11	12	19
Subcontractor exemption certificate frauds	–	48	146	92
Theft of payable orders and Giro cheques	27	34	211	188
Other	4	4	8	7
Total number of convictions	170	150	419	344
Total number of acquittals	11	12	9	20

Note: Due to rounding, totals do not always agree with sums of columns.

Source: Inland Revenue Annual Reports.

income, and, since the abolition of child tax allowances, the number of prosecutions for false claims to personal allowances, etc. has been even fewer.

The use of prosecution by the Inland Revenue is clearly highly selective and very cautious. Few of the prosecutions that are brought result in acquittal. In a study of Inland Revenue prosecutions for the submission of false accounts, Deane (1981) identified a number of factors that appeared to influence the Inland Revenue's decision to prosecute, including the existence of conspiracy or forgery, persistent incomplete disclosure after investigations had begun, and the involvement of accountants in the evasion. Most of the cases were ones where the evasion had been practised over a long period, but the amount of tax lost did not appear to be a major factor in the decision to prosecute.

For convicted offenders, Deane found that there was a high risk of imprisonment (67 per cent); suspended sentences were rarely used in his sample, partly because many of the cases studied pre-dated the introduction of suspended sentences in 1968. The average sentence of imprisonment for those jailed was seventeen months, and only one jail sentence exceeded three years.

VAT enforcement

The enforcement of VAT is based principally upon routine 'control' visits to registered traders and investigations of cases where fraudulent evasion is suspected. VAT 'ghosts' are not considered to be a major problem: a special exercise conducted in 1979 investigated all business in certain areas, and found that less than 1 per cent (owing on average less than £1,000 of VAT each) had failed to notify Customs and Excise of their existence (Keith Committee, para.2.4.2). About 1.4 million businesses are registered for VAT. If a further 1 per cent are unregistered, owing on average £1,000 each, the total loss of VAT due to 'ghosts' will be about £14 million, or about one-tenth of one per cent of total net VAT receipts.

When VAT was initially introduced it was envisaged that most traders would receive a control visit about once every three years. In practice the frequency of control visits is now lower than this, as a result of the Government's programme to reduce the size of the Civil Service. Since 1977/8 the resource effort devoted to VAT control visiting has declined from about 4,600 person-years to about 4,100 (Keith Committee, para.4.4.4), and the interval between control visits now exceeds three years for more than half of all VAT traders.

The yield from control visits has, however, risen in real terms due to a policy of greater selectivity in control visits, introduced following a review in 1978 of the administration of VAT. Operational research techniques are now used to identify where the risk of fraud or error is likely to be greatest. As a result of this greater selectivity the average underdeclaration of tax discovered per visit has risen from £152 in 1978/9 to £914 in 1983/4, which after allowing for inflation represents a rise of 260 per cent in real terms. Nevertheless, whilst selectivity has clearly improved the direct cost-effectiveness of control visits, it has reduced the degree of supervision experienced by other traders, especially smaller businesses with more 'straightforward' VAT affairs.

Certainly in direct cost:yield terms control visits for VAT may appear a relatively expensive enforcement technique. The cost of employing officers on VAT control was about £55 million in 1981/2 and £57 million in 1982/3, compared with yields of £155 million and £246 million respectively, a ratio of £3.60 recovered per £1 of enforcement expenditure. Nevertheless, it is clear that, as with PAYE Audit, some proportion of the cost of VAT control is the unavoidable cost of educating traders in the operation of the system, and the marginal yield from VAT control may not be fully reflected in these figures.

Each year VAT officers including those on control visits identify some 140,000 mis-statements of VAT liability (i.e. roughly one trader in ten). Most of these are the result of error, but a proportion are deliberate. The errors and many smaller suspected frauds are simply dealt with by assessment and recovery of the mis-stated tax; unlike direct tax assessments, these assessments bear no interest charge. Fraud investigations are generally only undertaken where the lost tax is significant—at least £250, and in practice £2,000 or more (Keith Committee, para.9.1.5).

Resource constraints generally limit the number of cases of suspected evasion of VAT that are investigated to about 1,000 a year. Investigators succeeded in obtaining sufficient evidence to support civil proceedings or penalties in about 600 of these cases per year. As the Keith Committee observed, this means that only one-half of one per cent of identified mis-statements of VAT liability are subject to penalties each year.

Where cases do result in penalties, however, Customs and Excise appears much more ready than the Inland Revenue to prosecute. About 100 VAT fraud prosecutions are brought annually, compared with about 500 'compounded settlements' involving interest surcharges.

Table 7.3, based on data in the Keith Committee Report, summarises the penalties incurred in VAT fraud cases investigated during financial years 1980/1 and 1981/2. There appears to be a tendency for cases involving larger arrears to result in prosecution rather than in a compounded settlement. It is difficult to assess how many cases of VAT fraud result in someone being imprisoned since some cases may involve more than one defendant. Data for 1981/2 in the Keith Committee Report (Keith Committee, Table 44) show that out of a total of 113 defendants in VAT fraud cases that year, sixty-one received a fine only, thirty-three received a suspended jail sentence, fourteen were jailed immediately for a period of one year or less, three received jail sentences of between one and two years, and two were sentenced under a Community Service Order. The probability of receiving an immediate custodial sentence if prosecuted for VAT fraud thus appears to be about 15 per cent; the average jail sentence for those imprisoned was about one year.

Conclusions

Conclusions about the effectiveness of the resources devoted to countering tax evasion—and hence about the deterrent effect of enforcement activities—are inevitably tentative, since it is difficult to assess the amount of tax evasion that remains undiscovered. The most effective approach would be a random compliance study, as reported by the US Internal Revenue Service (1979), but the Inland Revenue's powers do not currently permit this.

The Inland Revenue's enforcement work is substantially directed at the self-employed, but even so, only 3 per cent of returns from the self-employed are investigated each year. Tax inspectors believe that at least one-fifth of self-employed income tax returns probably understate income; in the cases actually investigated in 1980/1, the average tax evaded was around £1,000. If typical of self-employed taxpayers as a whole, these figures might point to a total loss of tax

TABLE 7.3

VAT Fraud Cases Concluded in 1980/1 and 1981/2: Penalties, annual averages

| | | | TOTAL | | | AVERAGE PER CASE | | |
	Number of cases	Arrears (£ thous.)	Monetary penalties (£ thous.)	Imprisonment (years)	Arrears (£ thous.)	Monetary penalties (£ thous.)	Imprisonment (years)
Cases resulting in:							
Prosecution	99	2,081	238	44	21.0	2.4	0.4[a]
Compounded settlement	511	3,778	2,386		7.4	4.7	
Arrears only	450	5,600			12.4		

[a] On average, forty-five persons were imprisoned for VAT fraud, with an average sentence of approximately one year.

Source: Keith Committee Report, 1983, vol. 1, pp. 176, 196.

on Schedule D incomes of the order of 10 per cent of the actual tax yield from self-employed taxpayers.

Much of the enforcement work of both Inland Revenue and Customs and Excise is combined with an 'educational' function, especially in the visits to businesses to supervise the functioning of PAYE and VAT collection. Increasingly, however, resources are being targeted to areas where high returns are anticipated. The cost-effectiveness of enforcement has been further enhanced—although the deterrent effect probably weakened—by a heavy reliance on settlements for extra tax and a very selective use of prosecution, especially by the Inland Revenue.

Chapter 8

Benefit fraud and the black economy

Since the War there has been a massive increase in the amount of money paid out by the Government in the form of unemployment and other social security benefits. This has reflected both a dramatic rise in the number of people claiming such benefits and an increase in the real value of the rates of benefit paid. Both these factors may have also promoted a higher level of fraudulent claims for benefit. The rise in the number of people claiming may have stretched the resources devoted to enforcement and may have reduced the risks involved in fraudulent claiming. The rise in real rates of benefit has increased the potential gains that can be made from benefit fraud, raising the incentive to benefit fraud.

Apart from anecdotage, there appears to be little evidence to back up claims of massive undetected benefit fraud. This chapter seeks to assemble what evidence there is, firstly about the incentives and scope for fraud afforded by the structure of the benefit system, secondly about the pattern of detected fraud and the effectiveness of the resources devoted to combating benefit abuse, and thirdly about the opportunities that may be open to unemployed people for 'working while claiming'.

The benefit system

The structure of the system of benefit payments has remained broadly along the lines established after the Beveridge Report in 1942, with unemployment benefit, sickness benefit and other 'contributory' benefits available to those of the unemployed who had previously paid National Insurance contributions, and supplementary benefit (formerly National Assistance) paid in cases of need, regardless of past contributions. Within this general framework, however, there have been a number of changes over the years. These have included the replacement of Family Allowances and the tax allowance for children by a system of child benefits in 1975, the introduction of Family Income Supplement (payable to families with low incomes from full-time work) in 1970, and, during the period between 1966 and 1982, the addition of an earnings-related supplement to unemployment benefits.

But whilst the benefit structure has remained much the same, the rates of the main benefits have risen sharply, and the numbers of people claiming social security and unemployment benefits have increased dramatically. In real terms (i.e. after allowing for inflation) the levels of both unemployment benefit and the basic rate of supplementary benefit doubled between 1950 and 1980, with most of the increase taking place before the mid-1960s. The increase in long-term supplementary benefit rates has been even greater—over $2\frac{1}{2}$ times since 1950. (See Figure 8.1.) While real wages have also risen considerably over the period, the growth in unemployment and supplementary benefit rates has been faster than that of wages.

The number of people claiming unemployment benefit has increased from 200,000 in 1960 to 700,000 in 1980 and nearly a million now. This has of course reflected the rise in the numbers unemployed, but it is clear that in recent years the increase in the number of unemployment benefit claimants has by no means matched the massive rise in unemployment. This is because of two features of the unemployment benefit system, that prevent many of today's unemployed from being eligible for unemployment benefit. Firstly, unemployment benefit entitlement depends on having accumulated the necessary contribution record—at least twenty-five weeks' National Insurance contributions during the relevant 'contributions' year. Many young people among the unemployed have never worked, and therefore have no National Insurance contribution record. Secondly, unemployment benefit is paid only for a maximum of fifty-two weeks; people who are unemployed for more than a year are switched to supplementary benefit instead. The rise in the unemployment level to over three million in 1984 has been accompanied by a sharp rise in the number unemployed for more than a year, and therefore claiming supplementary benefit rather than unemployment benefit.

By 1983 more than four million people were claiming supplementary benefit, compared with only about a million in 1948. Much of the rise has been in the number of unemployed claimants, from less than 100,000 in 1948 to about 1.8 million now. A further important factor was the rise during the 1950s and 1960s

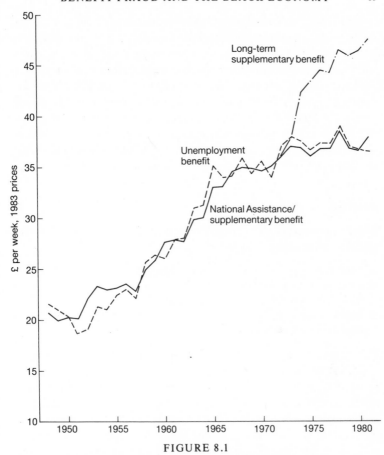

FIGURE 8.1

Real Levels of Unemployment Benefit and National
Assistance/Supplementary Benefit

in the number of pensioners qualifying for supplementary benefit,
from about 600,000 in 1948 to nearly two million by the late 1960s.

The rise in the number of people claiming unemployment benefit
and other social security benefits has obviously placed considerable
burdens on the administration of the system, including the
resources devoted to countering fraud. It may be that within a
larger total number of claimants it is easier for those determined to
defraud the system to escape detection.

While the number of Department of Health and Social Security

(DHSS) staff specifically devoted to countering benefit fraud has risen greatly during the past two decades, from less than two hundred in the mid-1960s to ten times that number now, the rise in staff numbers has not matched the dramatic rise in the number of claimants in the last five years. Between 1980 and 1983, while the number of unemployed claimants receiving supplementary benefit rose from 700,000 to 1.6 million and the total number of people claiming social security benefits administered by the DHSS rose by 40 per cent, the number of staff in DHSS local and regional offices employed directly on anti-fraud activities rose by only 8 per cent.

Detected frauds

Frauds connected with unemployment and social security benefits fall into three main categories:

- 'working while claiming', i.e. misrepresentation of employment status;
- other misrepresentation of personal circumstances (e.g. claiming for non-existent children, undeclared cohabitation, etc.);
- frauds connected with the payment mechanism (e.g. forgery or alteration of Giro cheques).

The relevance of each of these types of fraud to the black economy depends on the angle from which the subject is being approached. If what is at issue is the effectiveness of enforcement (i.e. how much benefit is being paid out to people who are not entitled to it) then all three types of fraud are relevant. On the other hand, if the main aspect of the black economy that is of interest is the extent to which it has caused a false impression of the true level of economic activity in the economy (i.e. the argument that actual gross domestic product (GDP) may be higher than measured GDP because the black economy is hidden and therefore does not get counted) then only the first type of fraud is relevant. Working while claiming requires that economic activity in the form of labour earnings and, possibly, output be concealed from the authorities, but making false claims about the number of dependent children or falsifying benefit cheques does not require that economic activity be hidden.

The rules governing the amount that can be earned while claiming benefit differ between unemployment benefit and supplementary benefit. Both permit a certain level of earnings without causing any reduction in benefit entitlement—the so-called 'earnings disregards'. In the case of unemployment benefit, part-time earnings of up to £2 a day are permitted without loss of benefit (75p a day before March 1982). The part-time work being done must not be the person's normal job, and must not affect their ability to take on a full-time job if one becomes available. If on any day earnings exceed the earnings disregard, then the whole amount of unemployment benefit for that day is lost. The rules for supplementary benefit are, at present, that £4 a week of a claimant's net weekly earnings and £4 a week of the earnings of the claimant's partner are disregarded. Pensioners face a higher earnings disregard, and single parents also receive more favourable treatment, based on a 'tapered' earnings disregard. Beyond the earnings disregard, benefits are reduced pound-for-pound with earnings.

The statistics of cases of benefit fraud discovered and considered for prosecution by the DHSS provide some indication of the importance in total detected fraud of working while claiming. Table 8.1 shows that about half of the social security offences considered for prosecution by the DHSS in 1983/4 come under the general heading of 'instrument of payment' offences (theft or alteration of Giro cheques, etc.). Apart from these instrument of payment offences, the total number of cases of benefit fraud considered in 1983/4 amounted to about 47,000 of which about

TABLE 8.1

Benefit Abuses Investigated by the DHSS, 1983/4

	Cases considered for proceedings	Prosecutions authorised
Benefit fraud, of which:	46,682	7,142
Working/earning by claimant	22,966	
Adult dependant earnings	5,874	
Cohabitation, fictitious desertion, etc.	3,267	
Other benefit fraud	14,575	
Instrument of payment fraud	49,008	894
Total	95,690	8,036

Source: DHSS figures.

STAFFORDSHIRE
POLYTECHNIC
LIBRARY

29,000 were cases involving undisclosed earnings. About 23,000 of the undisclosed earnings cases involved working while claiming on the part of the claimant; the remaining 6,000 were cases where the earnings of dependants had not been declared.

The authorities proceeded to prosecution in about 15 per cent of the cases of benefit fraud. Prosecution has become much less frequent since 1980 when, as a reaction to the high cost of prosecuting offenders, the DHSS decided to stop prosecuting claimants where the loss to the Department was less than £50. This threshold has since been raised, and the DHSS does not normally now prosecute for frauds involving less than £250. As a result, the number of prosecutions for benefit fraud has more than halved since 1980.

It is clear, however, that data on cases of detected benefit fraud cannot be used to infer the total extent of benefit fraud, both detected and undetected. It may be the case that nearly all benefit frauds are detected and are considered for prosecution; alternatively the offences detected may be only the 'tip of the iceberg' and there may be many other frauds that are undetected and do not come to light. The Fisher Committee on Abuse of Social Security Benefits, which reported in 1973, recommended that the DHSS should carry out a series of systematic surveys on random samples of all claimants in order to determine the true extent of benefit fraud. However, no such surveys have been undertaken, partly through reluctance to investigate innocent people where there was no ground for suspicion of fraud. In 1980 a Rayner Scrutiny Report on payments of benefit to unemployed people suggested that about 8 per cent of claimants were working while drawing benefit—implying that only about one in ten was detected. But in evidence to the Public Accounts Committee Sir Geoffrey Otton, Second Permanent Secretary at the DHSS, said that his Department had doubts about this estimate and thought that it may be too high: 'The trouble ... is that it is all speculation in the absence of hard evidence, and hard evidence can really only be obtained by grasping this nettle of a random investigation' (Public Accounts Committee, 1983, p. 58).

Hypothetical estimates of the extent of undetected fraud are of little use in determining the appropriate levels of resources to be devoted to enforcement work. The effectiveness of the existing anti-fraud work can, however, be measured in terms of the amount of benefit saved, and this can be related to the cost of resources used. Such a measure of the cost-effectiveness of resources devoted to enforcement is not, of course, an estimate of the effectiveness of marginal additional resources, but of the average. However, in areas where the marginal return is not believed to be significantly below the average—for example, where considerable amounts of suspected fraud are not investigated, owing to a lack of resources—significant differences in average effectiveness may nonetheless suggest where the balance of enforcement resources might be most effectively directed.

The first 'line of defence' against benefit fraud is the routine checking procedure carried out by local benefit office staff when new claims are first considered and when long-running cases come up for review. Most of the discrepancies identified at this stage are errors rather than deliberate fraud, but where fraud is suspected (or where, as frequently happens, the Department receives a 'tip-off' from a member of the public that a fraud is taking place) the case is referred to the specialist fraud section, based in the local office. Cases that can be resolved fairly easily (e.g. by checking with a claimant's employer) are settled by the local office fraud staff. More complex cases or those requiring in-depth investigation and surveillance are referred to a (growing) number of Special Investigators, who are based at regional level. A recent development has been the introduction of a third arm of the fraud investigation, Specialist Claims Control (SCC). Regionally based teams of investigators move from one local office area to another to investigate cases selected on the basis of predetermined criteria (e.g. 'unemployed construction workers', say) as being the most likely to contain fraud. The number of staff deployed on Specialist Claims Control has risen sharply since 1980, and by 1984 about 5 per cent of DHSS fraud staff were working in SCC teams. In total, about 2,200 staff were employed on fraud work at local and regional level by the DHSS. The Department of Employment, which is responsible for unemployment benefit, employed a further 650 or so staff on fraud work.

Since 1980, the DHSS has established cost criteria to monitor the effectiveness of the different anti-fraud and abuse specialists. The early results of this work, which estimated that the yield per head from SCC work was over three times that from local office fraud staff and that the overall annual saving per person engaged on fraud work was about £42,000, are now believed to have been rather high. More recent figures, based on an assessment of the likely duration of benefit savings made by the DHSS's Operational Research Service (Department of Health and Social Security, 1985) are shown in Table 8.2. Overall, the yield from investigation work per person employed in 1984/5 was about £47,000.

TABLE 8.2

Yield from Anti-Fraud Work, 1984/5

	Number of staff	1984/5 savings (£m)	Savings per person-year (£)
Local office fraud staff	1,513	58.2	38,500
Special Investigators	564	38.0	67,400
Specialist Claims Control	112	6.9	61,600
Total	2,189	103.1	47,100

Source: DHSS, 1985.

Staff and overhead costs associated with DHSS fraud investigation work are not known. However, it is clear that the ratio of savings to cost is unlikely to exceed 3:1 once overheads are taken into account, and could be less.

Opportunities for working while claiming

As with tax evasion, it is clear that information about the extent or pattern of detected fraud can at best be suggestive of the amount that remains undetected. Similarly, information about how the incentives and risks involved in benefit fraud or tax evasion have changed over time cannot be directly translated into estimates of the level of fraud or evasion actually taking place, although it might suggest the most likely direction of movement. But a lot depends on the moral attitudes both of claimants and of others, and on the opportunities for fraud that present themselves. The latter are particularly relevant in the case of working while claiming, where it is necessary to consider what groups of people there might be who, whilst apparently unable to find a job in the formal economy, might nonetheless be able to find sources of income outside it.

One group of the unemployed who may be working while claiming are people setting up in business on their own account. By no means all unemployed people setting up in business will carry on claiming benefit once they have begun to trade; many types of business are too conspicuous and rely on too much publicity for this to be possible. Other entrepreneurs may believe that to rely on the kinds of semi-clandestine business arrangement that is necessary to claim benefits successfully while working may signal the wrong kind of information to their potential customers. Customers may believe not only that they are entitled to get a cheap job, but also that they run a risk that the job may be shoddy. Perhaps there is a good reason that the workmen they are employing cannot find a job in the formal economy; even if there is not, the usual methods of finding out, through references, reputation and so forth, may run counter to the claimant's need to keep his business activities secret. These 'signalling' difficulties are likely to mean that working on own account while claiming will generally tend to involve businesses providing services to friends, relatives, and neighbours, rather than to the general public.

The problem of working while claiming by people setting up in business has in any case been seen more in terms of the disincentive to entrepreneurial activity resulting from benefit regulations, rather than any significant benefit loss that might be involved. The proportion of the unemployed who are likely to have the financial resources needed for most businesses and who have the necessary aptitude and skills is likely to be small. Since the introduction in 1983 of the Enterprise Allowance Scheme, the disincentive resulting from the loss of unemployment or supplementary benefit while starting up a business has been much reduced. The allowance provides financial assistance of £40 per week for the first twelve months of a new business, and is available both to the unemployed and to those who have been given notice of redundancy. About 50,000 individuals are currently benefiting under this scheme, of whom perhaps half would not have set up businesses without the allowance (Allen and Hunn, 1985). Of the remaining half, an unknown percentage might previously have comprised part of the black economy.

A second category of people who may be working while claiming are those in full-time employment. It would appear that this group, too, is unlikely to be numerous, and that most cases will eventually be detected, from cross-checking between tax and National Insurance records. Before the abolition of National Insurance cards, an immediate, physical control of working while claiming by employees existed, since the employee's National Insurance card had to be stamped by the employer every week, and was surrendered while unemployment benefit was being claimed. Since then, the control on working while claiming has become less direct, and is based on occasional cross-referral between tax and benefit records. Some limited scope for short periods of working-while-claiming exists, but this will eventually be detected, and more extensive working-while-claiming may be possible if a false name and National Insurance number can be supplied to the Inland Revenue.

The third, and possibly the most numerous, group amongst the working unemployed are unemployed people who fail to declare part-time or casual earnings in excess of the maximum permitted. The casual work obtained may be occasional employment in the unemployed person's normal trade or line of employment (e.g. an unemployed plumber who occasionally does odd plumbing jobs for friends and neighbours), or it may be casual employment in another trade (generally the typical poorly paid casual employments such as bar-work, cleaning, etc.).

The percentage of the unemployed who are able to obtain occasional work of the first sort will be quite low. Most of the unemployed are poorly equipped for work in the black economy, having generally lower skill levels than those in employment or skills that are typically not in demand in the black economy. For example, there are likely to be few opportunities for the unemployed former coal-miners in the north-east to use their skills in casual jobs; moreover, such opportunities as do arise will be shared amongst a large number of former miners with the same skills.

The group of the unemployed who obviously do have skills in demand in the black economy are unemployed skilled workers in the building trades. In May 1982, the most recent month for which an industry breakdown of unemployment has been published, about 390,000 workers in the construction industry were registered unemployed. Supposing—for the purpose of illustration—that as many as half of these unemployed construction workers were in fact able to obtain casual work for twenty hours a week, for eight months of the year, this would be equivalent to 65,000 full-time jobs, or less than 7 per cent of total construction industry employment.

The majority of the unemployed do not, however, have skills that are in demand in the black economy. They also have a much narrower range of social contacts than people with jobs, and hence a much lower chance of hearing about opportunities for casual work. In a survey, Trew and Kilpatrick (1984) found that unemployed men spent as much as 73 per cent of their waking hours at home, and only 15 per cent of their time in the company of people other than members of their family. Six times as many of the unemployed reported that their social contacts had been curtailed as a result of unemployment as reported that they had increased.

Occasional work in the black economy may also require access to tools and facilities which those who are in employment can 'borrow' from their main jobs. This puts the unemployed at a considerable disadvantage in the black economy: 'In the battle for informal economy employment the unemployed are up against not only their fellows but also the employed who, because of their resource base in the formal economy, are able to operate a totally irrational price structure, making them unassailably powerful competitors' (Henry, 1982).

Those of the unemployed most able to find occasional work will thus be those whose skills are in demand in the black economy, and who need neither significant amounts of equipment nor much working capital. The demand for such work will tend to be affected by general business conditions in the local area. Gershuny and Pahl (1979) observe that the scope for occasional work while claiming benefit will be least in areas of high unemployment: 'Those regions and local areas with the highest levels of unemployment are frequently those with the poorest social infrastructure, and the very fact of high unemployment means relative local poverty and restricted markets for products and services'. As Coffield, Borrill, and Marshall (1983) remarked, 'If your neighbours are all on social security, few of them can afford to have their windows cleaned'.

Conclusions

The number of people claiming unemployment benefit and other social security benefits has risen massively in the past decade, but the numbers of staff engaged on anti-fraud work at the DHSS and the Department of Employment have risen more slowly. There has been a growing move towards the use of specialist anti-fraud teams, and the identification and investigation of categories of claimants with the greatest opportunities for fraudulent 'working while claiming'.

It is likely that few of the unemployed will have either the skills or the financial resources to be actively engaged in business on their own account, and cross-checking through National Insurance records restricts the scope for working as an employee while claiming benefit. It is likely that most of the working while claiming by the unemployed will involve relatively low casual earnings, except for a few groups such as unemployed construction workers whose skills may be in greater demand in the black economy.

In comparison with tax evasion, more is spent on enforcement per pound recovered, and considerably greater recourse is had to prosecution of offenders. One pound spent on enforcement by the DHSS appears to recover no more than about £3 of benefit, compared with an average of about £6 from income tax investigation work.

Part III
Measuring the black economy

Chapter 9

Measuring the black economy

Measuring economic activity that is illicit or has been concealed from the revenue or social security authorities presents particular problems. Many of the sources routinely used to compile official statistics are connected with the administration of the tax and social security system, and will not include any activity that has been successfully concealed. Other official surveys may also be treated with suspicion by people active in the black economy, even if the survey has no direct connection with the revenue or social security authorities. People may be cautious about identifying themselves as tax evaders in any official survey, regardless of any assurances that may be given about the confidentiality of individual data, for fear that, nonetheless, the information might somehow be communicated back to the revenue or social security authorities.

One response open to people active in the black economy when faced with an official survey is to reply, but to adjust their answers so as to conceal their black economy trading. Gutmann (1979a) believes that this happens frequently: 'Put bluntly, plenty of respondents [to the US Current Population Survey] lie; they lie consistently, and they lie with good reason'. Another possible response, to a voluntary survey, is simply not to reply at all. Most official surveys have a considerable percentage of non-respondents (in the Family Expenditure Survey, for example, the non-response rate is about 30 per cent), and the tax evader is unlikely to attract attention by refusing to respond to any official survey. The extent to which either of these reactions to official surveys occurs is, of course, impossible to prove. Gutmann's argument certainly seems plausible enough, and at the very least it must be anticipated that some participants in the black economy may fail to respond to surveys, and others may 'adjust' their replies, where they think that truthful replies might reveal their activity in the black economy. It is not, however, impossible that some percentage may respond, and respond truthfully to all but the most direct questions about their own tax evasion. It is, however, difficult to gain any impression of how important this group may be.

Official surveys might thus be expected to be very unreliable in the direct information they yield about the black economy. There are, moreover, indications that the wariness of people active in the black economy about surveys extends well beyond surveys conducted by government statistical offices. A Social Science Research Council (SSRC) survey of second-job holding conducted in 1971, for example, found that as the questions asked about second jobs became more detailed the response rate declined. About half the respondents who initially admitted they 'did extra work in their spare time' did not answer a later question about whether any tax deductions were made from their second-job earnings. Part of the fall-off in response will have been because respondents realised that later questions were not applicable to the work referred to in their initial answer (e.g. because the work was unpaid), but it also seems possible that some respondents stopped answering the questions for fear of incriminating themselves (Brown, Levin, Rosa, and Ulph, 1984). An even more striking reluctance to reply was found by Keenan and Dean (1980) who were surveying taxpayers' attitudes to tax evasion. They found that an adequate response rate could only be achieved by guaranteeing and demonstrating the complete anonymity of the replies, by conducting the survey in a public place and asking respondents to place their written (and completely anonymous) replies in a sealed box.

Such extreme caution—verging perhaps on paranoia—contrasts sharply with the enthusiasm with which many pub bores appear prepared to regale even complete strangers with tediously detailed anecdotes about their transactions in the black economy and their views about taxation. An appropriately designed survey technique should surely be able to harness some of this pent-up confessional energy, to shed light on at least some parts of the black economy.

Customers in the black economy

One promising angle might be to talk to the black economy's customers about their transactions in the black economy. Customers, having broken no law themselves, are likely to be far less inhibited than sellers and producers in the black economy, and have less reason to lie. Some customers may still be wary, nonetheless, and want to avoid incriminating a friend or relative who had evaded tax; others may be uncertain whether their part in the transaction is, in fact, totally legal, and may be cautious for this reason. But many people are clearly happy to talk—in general terms at least—about tradesmen they have encountered who are apparently evading tax, and appropriate survey design and careful interviewing could maximise this co-operation.

One detailed example of research along these lines was a study in Detroit reported by Ferman and Berndt (1981). This surveyed about 300 households in 1977, focusing on the use of irregular and social sources as an alternative to the regular economy in obtaining common home-related and personal services. They found that 60 per cent of the services that households reported using were secured through the 'social economy'. They were produced within the household itself or provided by friends, relatives, neighbours, or co-workers without monetary payment. Of the services, 10 per cent were purchased through the black economy and 30 per cent through regular suppliers. Over half the households surveyed (51 per cent) had purchased at least one service in the black economy. The services that were most frequently purchased in the black economy were lawn-mowing, painting and decorating, paneling, carpentry, baby-sitting, and childcare—although the majority of households nonetheless obtained these services for free through the social economy. Ferman and Berndt concluded that the black economy 'was generally utilised for services that most people would otherwise secure without monetary payment through their social channels, and which are usually not provided by regular firms and businesses ... [it] fills an intermediate position between the regular market economy and "do-it-yourself" activities'.

A similar research approach was adopted by Pahl (1984) in a study of work and service provision in 1981 among a sample of 730 households on the Isle of Sheppey in Kent. The survey sought information on the sources of labour that the households drew on to get certain tasks done. The forty-one tasks studied covered a wide range of individual activities in the broad areas of house maintenance, home improvement and decoration, housework, domestic production (making clothes, home-brewing, etc.), car maintenance, and childcare. Households were asked what sources of labour they had used to get these tasks done and whether they had paid for the work. The sources of labour were classified into four groups: unpaid work done within the household, unpaid work done by friends or relatives, paid work done by friends or relatives, and paid work done by firms. The third category corresponds quite closely to moonlighting, and it is a reasonable guess that few of the payments would have been declared for tax. The fourth category includes the formal economy, although it was not possible to tell whether the firms involved declared all their income to the tax authorities. Pahl found that informally paid labour of friends or relatives was used for only a relatively limited number of tasks—mainly painting, plastering, domestic cleaning, and some car maintenance. Apart from window cleaning, where informally paid labour was widely used, informal paid work by friends and relatives tended even so to be relatively infrequent; at least twice as many households employed firms to do painting as employed friends or relatives, and for car maintenance the percentage of paid work done by friends or relatives was even lower—less than one-fifth. Nearly all paid house improvement and renovation work (as opposed to routine maintenance) was done by firms rather than moonlighters.

Neither Pahl's work nor the Detroit study covered the full range of goods and services that might be produced in the black economy. But the provision of services to households does seem, from the pattern of anecdotage if nothing else, to be the area where 'black' activity is most widespread. The considerations outlined in the previous chapters would confirm this: evasion of value added tax (VAT) is more likely on sales to households than on sales to other firms (which can generally claim VAT back on purchases) or on sales to the government sector. Retail sales of goods to households are unlikely to involve much VAT evasion, because the low margins in much of the retail sector provide little scope to 'hide' off-the-books transactions within the balance-sheet whilst at the same time claiming back VAT on the total value of wholesale purchases. Services, in contrast, involve a higher ratio of value added to inputs, which gives more scope for fraudulently understating value added; moreover, services to households are often supplied by small firms, which face fewer problems of managerial control than large firms if they try to evade VAT. At the same time, the relatively low capital requirements in the household service sector will tend to give greater scope in this area for own-account working by the unemployed and moonlighting by those in employment.

Household spending in the black economy—an estimate

The pattern of household expenditures revealed in the Family Expenditure Survey gives a broad indication of the percentage of spending that could be devoted to black economy services. An average household spent £142.59 per week in 1983 of which the largest amounts were on food, housing, and transport and vehicles (Table 9.1). Total expenditure on services (excluding transport) was somewhat higher than that shown under the 'services' item in Table 9.1, since spending on repairs of goods and appliances, meals out, and payments to contractors for repairs and decoration are included elsewhere in the table, but nonetheless it was under 15 per cent of total spending. Table 9.2 shows much more detail about

TABLE 9.1

Average Household Expenditure, 1983

	Average household expenditure (£ per week)
Housing	23.99
Fuel, light, and power	9.22
Food	29.56
Alcoholic drink	6.91
Tobacco	4.21
Clothing and footwear	10.00
Durable household goods	10.26
Other goods	10.81
Transport and vehicles	20.96
Services	16.09
Miscellaneous	0.58
Total	142.59
Average weekly expenditure per person	53.65

Source: Family Expenditure Survey, 1983, Table 5.

TABLE 9.2

Household Spending on Typical Black Economy Items

	Total spending on item (£ per week)	Assumed spending in black economy (£ per week)
Structural alterations and additions to dwellings	2.39	0.72
Payments to contractors for repairs, maintenance, and decorations	0.94	0.28
Ice-cream and iced lollies	0.19	0.06
Meals out (tips element in black economy)	2.92	0.29
Repairs to TVs, radios, etc.	0.08	0.02
Repairs to gas and electric appliances	0.20	0.06
Vehicle repairs	1.63	0.49
Taxi fares	0.30	0.09
Contribution towards cost of travel in friend's car, etc. (100% in black economy)	0.08	0.08
Other travel and transport (removals, etc.)	0.12	0.04
Theatres, sporting events, and other entertainment	1.14	0.17
Domestic help, etc.	0.53	0.16
Hairdressing, manicure, etc.	0.98	0.29
Repairs to footwear, etc.	0.28	0.08
Laundry, cleaning, and dyeing	0.23	0.07
Private tuition and other educational fees	0.51	0.15
Cash gifts and tips not allocated elsewhere (tips element in black economy)	1.00	0.30
Miscellaneous expenditure on services (e.g. newspaper advertisements, public baths, etc.)	0.78	0.12
Total, these items	£14.30	£3.47
● as % of total household expenditure	10%	2.4%

Source: Family Expenditure Survey, 1983, Annex A.

spending on individual services frequently thought to be provided through the black economy—repairs to vehicles and household appliances, taxi journeys, domestic help, building repairs, painting and decorating, hairdressing, and so on. Some of the categories are quite heterogeneous, and some include charges for services provided by local authorities or large companies. In total including these categories, household expenditure on services where the black economy may be significant averaged £14.30 per week.

Neither the Detroit study nor Pahl's research on service provision in Sheppey would support the view that more than a quarter of the total expenditure on these services was in the black economy rather than the formal economy. Allowing for the possibility that some black economy purchases were 'disguised' by the respondents to protect their suppliers and that some more transactions may have taken place in the black economy without their customers realising, a figure of 30 per cent for black economy provision of these services might be a conceivable, though high, estimate. A similar percentage might be reached by considering the conceivable upper bound of off-the-books activity that could be successfully concealed by the average of apparently legitimate businesses.

Applying this percentage to the figures in Table 9.2, and a lower percentage of 15 per cent to the heterogeneous categories, gives an average expenditure on black economy services by households of about £3.47 per week in 1983. In other words, *no more than 2½ per cent of the spending of an average household in 1983 is likely to have been direct spending on goods and services from the black economy*.

Of course, this 'informed guess' of the possible level of household spending on black economy goods and services by no means covers the whole range of black economy production. But it does cover the services where the black economy is believed to be most important, and it does serve to put into perspective the implications of some of the larger estimates of the extent of the black economy. Matthews and Rastogi (1985), for example, concluded from analysis of monetary trends that the black economy amounted to 14.5 per cent of gross domestic product (GDP) in 1983. This would imply that GDP in the black economy amounted to some £45 billion, and that the average household was spending on black economy goods and services between £2,000 and

£2,500 annually—or perhaps £40 per week, clearly well above the figures in Table 9.2, and extending well beyond the products normally associated with the black economy.

Other measurement approaches

The major problem with relying on information from customers to gauge the extent of the black economy is that customers themselves may sometimes be unaware that they are buying goods and services from the black economy. This is likely to be the case where proprietors of apparently legitimate businesses conceal a proportion of their income from the Inland Revenue. They may have no need to let their customers know that they are trading off-the-books, and indeed may not decide until the end of the year which transactions to conceal and which to declare for tax. At all events, where there is no need for the customer to know that the trader is not declaring the transaction for tax, the customer is unlikely to be told.

Estimating the full extent of the black economy, including tax evasion by apparently legitimate businesses, requires a more indirect approach. Black economy activity may leave 'traces' elsewhere in the economy, which may make it possible to assess indirectly the scale of hidden incomes. Two broad classes of indirect measurement have been employed by researchers: cash measurement methods, which try to assess the scale of the black economy from the relationship between money in circulation and the level of economic activity; and methods based on income/expenditure discrepancies, either at the aggregate level or in data about individual households.

The first use of trends in cash demand to draw inferences about the changes in the level of underground economic activity was in the late 1950s by Cagan, who studied the sharp rise in cash demand in war-time America and interpreted it as being the cash needed for (unrecorded) transactions in the war-time black market (Cagan, 1958). More recently Gutmann has been an enthusiastic advocate of the use of cash demand as an indicator of the black economy. He has drawn attention to the 'amazing sums' that people hold in currency and has contended that it 'lubricates a vast amount of non reported income and non reported work and employment, a whole subterranean economy, untaxed and substantially ignored'

(Gutmann, 1977). Estimates of the scale of the black economy based on this approach vary widely, and the method has been used to derive some of the largest estimates of the total extent of activity in the black economy. Using this approach, Matthews and Rastogi (1985) have, for example, estimated that the UK black economy may now approach about 15 per cent of GDP.

Chapter 10 describes the various measurement approaches based on the amount of cash in circulation, and considers whether any firm conclusions can be drawn from cash-based estimates of the size of the black economy in the United Kingdom.

Chapter 11 examines the evidence about the scale of the black economy that can be obtained from the discrepancy between the national accounts estimates of total incomes and total expenditures in the UK economy. The estimates of total expenditures are believed to be largely unaffected by the existence of the black economy, but the statistics of total incomes are based on incomes declared to the Inland Revenue. The gap between the two, amounting to up to about 4 per cent of gross domestic product, will reflect measurement errors in both incomes and expenditures, but its trend may provide an indication of the amount of income that is concealed from the UK tax authorities. Chapter 11 considers whether this discrepancy is indeed an adequate measure of the overall black economy. It examines also whether the black economy might not affect the national accounts in more complex ways, with the result both that the discrepancy between aggregate incomes and expenditures may no longer be a useful indicator of the level of income concealed from the tax authorities, and that the overall accuracy of the national accounts may be compromised by errors in both the income and expenditure measures of GDP.

Chapter 12 also looks for evidence of discrepancies between incomes and expenditures, but at the microeconomic level, using survey data for individual households, rather than at the level of the whole economy. The annual Family Expenditure Survey contains information on the incomes and expenditures of a sample of about 7,000 households, based largely on interviews and a diary record of spending by household members during the two-week survey period. Chapter 12 describes two possible ways in which this information can be used to try to identify households that appear to be able to afford a more affluent lifestyle than could be afforded on the incomes they declare. The first approach, used by Dilnot and Morris (1981), looked for households where total spending was significantly greater than total income, and where there was no obvious reason in the family's circumstances that could account for the difference. The second approach reported in Chapter 12 is a new one, and is based on a comparison of the consumption patterns of employee and self-employed households at various levels of household income. Self-employed households are likely to have considerably more scope for evading tax than employee households, and the figures for self-employed households' incomes may therefore understate the true level of their income by much more than the corresponding figures for employee households do. As is indeed found in Chapter 12, the self-employed households would then appear to spend more than similar employee households with the same level of reported income. Their higher living standard would betray higher incomes than they had admitted.

Chapter 10

Evidence from the demand for cash

with Michael Kell

The 'cash' approach to measuring the size of the black economy is based on the notion that black economy transactions are made in cash to avoid detection. This increases the demand for notes and coin above what would be expected from the level of activity in the formal economy. Estimates of the scale of the black economy might then be derived from the demand for notes and coin that cannot be explained by economic activity in the formal economy.

Cash transactions

Cash transactions are by no means confined to the black economy. The vast majority of transactions in the formal economy are made in cash: estimates by the Inter-Bank Research Organisation (IBRO), quoted in Bank of England (1982) at p. 522, suggest that only about three-and-a-half billion of the more than fifty billion payments made every year in the United Kingdom are made by means other than cash. The great majority of transactions are of low value: in 1981 over 70 per cent were for sums less than £1, and virtually all of these would have been made in cash. The rate of use of cheques and other non-cash media increases as the value of the transaction rises. In 1981 cash was used for about three-quarters of transactions (by value) between £3 and £10, compared with only about a third of transactions of more than £100 (Bank of England, 1982, p. 524).

For a considerable portion of the population, wages too are paid in cash. According to IBRO research (IBRO, 1982), 42 per cent of the working population in 1981 were paid weekly in cash, compared with 15 per cent paid weekly by other methods (cheque and bank Giro credit), and 38 per cent paid monthly.

As these figures show, cash is widely used throughout the formal economy. Cash use in the black economy is less well documented. It has frequently been taken for granted that black economy transactions are made entirely in cash, to reduce the risk of detection. Certainly much of the anecdotage uses cash payment as an indicator of 'black' activity. The plumber, for example, who requests every payment in cash (or offers a discount for cash rather than cheque payments) is almost universally assumed to be fiddling his tax. While in many instances this may indeed be the case, a preference for cash payments is by no means confined to those evading tax. Cash payments may be more convenient, obviating the need for trips to the bank, and above all they are final payment. Cheques can bounce; notes and coin cannot. It is interesting to speculate how frequently a demand for cash payment may have been interpreted by the customer as evidence of tax evasion when in fact the primary motive may have been suspicion of the customer's creditworthiness.

Equally, there is little reason to believe that black economy transactions are made exclusively in cash. The use of barter would seem to have the same advantage as cash, in that it can leave no trace for the taxman to uncover. In many instances, moreover, it would seem to have a degree of legal ambiguity (are barter transactions subject to tax, and if so at what value?) which would reduce the risks of prosecution or penalty as well as the risks of detection. Nevertheless, despite these attractions, barter is unlikely ever to account for more than a small proportion of all transactions, since it depends on the coincidence of finding parties to the transaction with exactly matching supplies and demands. Whilst parsons prepared to conduct a wedding in exchange for a side of pork may be the stuff of good gossip, not all parsons may have a taste for pork, and civil servants and computer technicians have no pork to exchange.

Cheques, too, may well be used for some black economy transactions. Cheques made payable to 'cash' and uncrossed cheques need not be passed through the payee's bank account and involve no greater risk of detection than cash payments. Also, the extent to which transactions even when passed through a bank account increase the risk of detection of a modest level of 'black' activity can easily be overstated. There would appear to be positive advantages for some black economy traders in accepting payment by cheque to the same extent as corresponding legitimate traders would. There is always, of course, the risk that a request for payment in cash may be made to the wrong person. But, in addition, some customers may be suspicious of goods and services that they know to be black economy goods and services. Quite realistically, they may fear that the lack of documentation may affect their ability to obtain redress for bad workmanship or defective products. A black economy trader in these circumstances might well not reveal himself as such, might accept payment by cheque and provide all the normal documentation, but could nevertheless later conceal a portion of his business from the tax authorities, perhaps by false accounting, with a reasonable hope of avoiding detection.

The view that payments in cash could be an indicator of the extent of black economy activity is, however, reflected in the 1976 survey reported by Miller (1979). This asked passers-by in the street about various services frequently believed to be associated with the black economy, such as window-cleaning, painting and decorating, home-help, etc. Over half of the services that respondents said they had paid for 'in the last month or so' had cost less than £5, and only 12 per cent had cost more than £50. Payments made in cash (rather than by cheque) were analysed by amount of payment. Low-value payments were nearly all made in cash, with 95 per cent of payments of £5 or less being cash payments. As the value of the transaction rose, the percentage paid in cash declined: 44 per cent of payments between £5 and £50 and only 32 per cent of payments where the amount exceeded £50 were made in cash.

The most striking thing about these figures is not in fact the high proportion of the payments made in cash, but rather how closely the pattern of payments matches that in the economy as a whole. Not only does the percentage paid in cash decline as the transaction value rises, but also the percentages reported by Miller for transactions of different values are very close to the percentages reported by the Bank of England (1982, p. 524). Once allowance is made for the rough doubling of the price level between 1976 and 1981, it seems that cash is used no more widely in payment for these services than for transactions as a whole.

The Bank of England figures, for example, show that a little over 30 per cent of the value of transactions exceeding £100 were made in cash in 1981, compared with Miller's figure of 32 per cent of the number of transactions exceeding £50 in 1976. For transactions between £10 and £100 the Bank of England data suggest that at least 40 per cent by value were paid in cash, which is close to Miller's estimate that 44 per cent of transactions between £5 and

£50 in 1976 were paid in cash. Indeed, if anything the Bank of England data understate the percentage of transactions paid in cash compared with Miller's data, since the Bank of England percentages are percentages by value, which give a lower weighting to lower-value transactions of which a higher percentage involve cash. Miller's '£5 or less' category cannot be precisely compared with the Bank of England data, which do not include transactions below £3. Such transactions form a large percentage of all transactions, and are nearly all paid in cash. It does not seem that Miller's figure for this category is significantly out of line with the percentage of transactions of this value made in cash in the economy as a whole.

It would be unwise to draw firm conclusions about cash use in the black economy from a single survey. But Miller's data do suggest that even in those service sector activities where the black economy is widely believed to be rife, cash use is not markedly different from cash use in the economy as a whole. This may of course imply that the black economy is smaller than popular anecdotage would have us believe. Alternatively, it may simply mean that black economy transactions do not involve a higher use of cash than similar transactions elsewhere in the economy. People may pay their window-cleaners in cash, but this is as much a reflection of the low value of the transaction as of anything else. Equally, larger payments both for the services studied by Miller and for other large transactions are less often made in cash. Perhaps in view of this it would be wise to be cautious about identifying transactions in cash too closely with transactions in the black economy.

Cash holdings

Between 1960 and 1980 the total value of cash held by the public in the UK rose nearly fivefold. However, this rise was entirely due to inflation. After allowing for inflation the real value of cash in circulation stayed broadly constant during the 1960s and early 1970s, and has since started to decline rapidly (Figure 10.1). By 1980 the real value of cash held was about 12 per cent lower than in 1960.

Cash is held for two main purposes—for use as a means of payment in buying and selling, and as a store of value. Holdings of

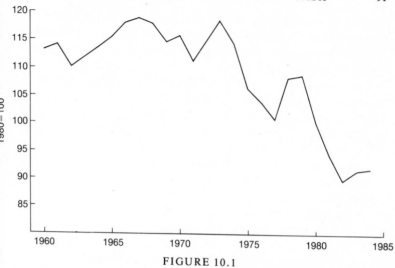

FIGURE 10.1

Real Value of Notes and Coin in Circulation with the Public

cash for transaction purposes would be generally expected to move in line with the value of transactions; however, during the 1960s and 1970s cash holdings declined in real terms while the real value of consumers' expenditure nearly doubled. It is clear that there were considerable economies in cash holdings for transaction purposes, partly reflecting innovations in payments technology, such as the introduction and wider use of cheques and credit cards, and partly perhaps reflecting more economical management of the cash held by companies in tills, for wage payments, etc.

A number of aspects of this process of financial innovation can be seen in surveys of consumer payments and financial behaviour. While the vast majority of transactions are still made in cash, there has been an appreciable rise in the number of non-cash transactions since the mid-1970s. 30 per cent of payments of £3 or more were made by cheque in 1981, compared with only 19 per cent of similar transactions five years earlier. Other non-cash means of payment (direct debit, standing orders, credit cards, etc.) accounted for a further 20 per cent of payments in 1981, compared with 13 per cent in 1976 (Bank of England, 1982, p. 522). The percentage of the population having a bank current account rose by over 60 per cent during the 1970s, and the number of credit cards issued increased sixfold. Cash dispensers, which improve the public's access to cash and therefore may promote greater efficiency in the holding of cash for transaction purposes, have become widely used: the number installed increased by about four times over the decade (Johnston, 1984, pp. 9–10).

The increasing use of credit transfers to pay wages and salaries has enabled companies to economise their holdings of cash too. Only 42 per cent of people were paid weekly in cash in 1981, compared with 58 per cent five years earlier and 75 per cent at the end of the 1960s (Bank of England, 1982, p. 521). Company cash holdings now account for only about 8 per cent of total notes and coin in circulation outside the monetary sector.

The data in Figure 10.1 would seem to suggest that the pace of financial innovation has accelerated during the early 1980s. The real value of notes and coin held by the public fell by over 16 per cent between 1979 and 1983, while consumers' expenditure remained broadly constant. One factor underlying this rapid reduction in real cash holdings would seem to be the opportunity cost of holding cash—the interest that could be earned if the money was held in some interest-bearing form rather than as cash. Interest rates rose sharply from 6 per cent in 1978 to 12 per cent in 1979 and 14 per cent in 1980, and although they have fallen back considerably since then they remain much higher in real terms than in the 1970s. The high opportunity cost of holding cash (coupled with the greater use of savings media such as building society accounts) might have reduced the amount of savings held in cash. But high interest rates will also have encouraged companies and individuals to economise still further in the use of cash for transaction purposes too.

Cash holdings and the black economy

Despite the fact that the amount of cash held by the UK public remained broadly constant in real terms for most of the 1960s and 1970s while the real value of transactions rose, and despite the fact that cash holdings have fallen in real terms since about 1975, some writers have tried to interpret the data on the aggregate use of cash as evidence of a large, or even of a *growing*, black economy in recent years. This work follows in the footsteps of a considerable body of work for the United States interpreting aggregate monetary statistics as evidence of illicit black economy transactions. But, as will be seen from the review of these cash indicators in the following subsections, the evidence for the UK is far from convincing. Some of the indicators that have been used to show a growing black economy in the United States appear to point to a rapidly shrinking one in the United Kingdom. Only by being very selective about the monetary indicators used and by ignoring those that point to the opposite conclusion is it possible to show any kind of stable pattern of black economy growth emerging from the analysis of cash statistics.

Furthermore, most of the cash indicators of the size of the black economy are liable to reflect other changes in the pattern of cash holdings, in addition to those resulting from changes in the level of black economy transactions. As the last two sections have shown, patterns of cash use have been in considerable turmoil during the past decade, reflecting the rapid pace of financial innovation. Inflation and rising real incomes are also likely to have affected cash demand. It would be surprising if it were an easy matter to distinguish the effects of these factors and the effects of black economy growth on cash demand. At the very least, it would be implausible to interpret the changes in indicators of aggregate monetary holdings as a reflection only of changes in the amount of cash being used in the black economy, without attempting to assess the extent to which financial innovations may also have influenced the same indicators.

The following subsections review, in turn, a number of the monetary indicators that have, at various times, been held to indicate the scale of the black economy, either in the US or in the UK. While some show a greater degree of sophistication—or, at any rate, technical complexity—than others, none make explicit allowance for other factors, such as the extent of financial innovation, that may have had a large influence on cash demand.'

per capita *cash holdings*

The simplest observation about cash holdings, and perhaps the most puzzling, is the high *per capita* value of notes and coin held by the public. Gutmann (1977) has referred to the 'incredibly, indeed suspiciously, large amounts of cash in circulation'. In 1983 the aggregate value of notes and coin in circulation with the public in the UK was about £11.7 billion, or around £205 per head of population. Company cash holdings are thought to account for less than a tenth of this (Johnston, 1984, p. 9) and a certain proportion could be held abroad, but these figures would seem to suggest that an average family of four could be holding as much as £750 of cash.

It is absurd to suggest that a family of four needs to hold anywhere near as much cash as this for transaction purposes, whether in the formal economy or in the black economy. Average household expenditure per person (including cheque transactions) in 1983 was little more than £50 per week (Family Expenditure Survey, 1983). With a weekly cycle of cash holdings, either from weekly trips to the bank or from weekly wage payments, and a steady pattern of household expenditure, the average value of cash held for transaction purposes per household would be only about £100. Clearly other factors must account for a considerable proportion of the cash held by the public.

Cash balances of companies trading 'off-the-books' and the wads of 'used fivers' handed over in criminal transactions could explain some of the remainder, although these operations would have to be on a quite astronomical scale to account for all of the difference. Other factors could be holdings of UK notes and coin abroad, and savings held in the form of cash. This latter use of cash is poorly documented, though conceivably quite substantial. To many people, of course, it may seem a wilfully expensive way of holding savings, since high interest can be earned with only a negligible sacrifice of liquidity in building societies or bank deposit accounts. However, given the number of people who appear to hold balances way in excess of transaction needs in non-interest-bearing bank current accounts, it is quite possible that some people still hold large savings in the form of cash.

Before the high level of *per capita* cash holding is taken as evidence of an extensive black economy it is necessary to assess the amount that may be being used for savings and other purposes. Neither for the UK nor for the US has this been done, and it cannot be attempted here. Suffice it to say that the margin of error surrounding such an assessment is likely to be considerably greater than the amount of cash in use in the black economy, even if the black economy were as extensive as 15 per cent of gross domestic product (GDP). For suppose cash held for transaction purposes in the formal economy per family of four to be £100 and cash required for the black economy to be a further £30 (assuming the transactions velocity of cash in the black economy to be half that in the formal economy). Then a total of £130 cash per household is being held for transaction purposes, and the remaining £600 or so of cash per household needs to be accounted for, in the form of savings and other uses. A 5 per cent error in estimating this quantity would be sufficient to absorb all the cash we have assumed is in the black economy. Put another way, *per capita* cash holdings are far too large to be accounted for simply by the black economy. Our uncertainty about the amount of cash that is held as savings and for other purposes makes it difficult to draw any conclusions at all about the scale of the black economy from data about *per capita* cash holdings.

High *per capita* cash holdings are a phenomenon not confined to the UK. Indeed, as Table 10.1 shows, the UK had the lowest *per capita* holding of cash out of eleven industrial countries in 1981, and one of the lowest holdings of cash in relation to consumption expenditures. Perhaps some very small part of these differences could be accounted for by differences in the scale of the black economy in the countries shown. But all of the difference cannot be, because then in some of the countries shown the black economy would exceed the size of the measured economy. Again, without an

TABLE 10.1

Cash Ratios, 1981

	Cash per head ($)	Ratio of cash to consumers' expenditure (%)
UK	339	7
Belgium	975	16
Canada	367	6
France	549	8
West Germany	604	10
Italy	455	12
Japan	722	13
Netherlands	628	11
Sweden	856	12
Switzerland	1,977	21
US	552	7

Source: Bank of England, 1982, p. 525.

adequate evaluation of the other reasons for the level of *per capita* cash holdings it is difficult to reach any conclusions at all about the relative scale of the black economy from these indicators.

Circulation of large notes

The monetary indicator of the black economy that has attracted popular interest most readily has been the apparent 'disproportionate growth' in the circulation of high-denomination notes. Ross (1978) observed a more rapid growth in the circulation of $100 bills in the US than of other denominations of notes. He argued that this was due to the growth of illicit transactions, for which high-denomination notes, rather than cheques, were used, so as to avoid detection.

In the UK, according to Freud (1979), the corresponding growth in circulation of high-denomination notes has been 'far faster': 'Between 1972 and 1978 the aggregate value of £10 and £20 notes in circulation grew by 470 per cent, while the growth in the aggregate value of all British notes rose by only 110 per cent. Inflation and increased consumer spending accounts for only a small proportion of the increase, for over the same six years, consumer expenditure at current prices rose by only 140 per cent. As a proportion of all notes, the two higher denomination notes increased from 15 per cent in 1972 to just over 40 per cent in 1978'.

This approach has, however, been the subject of vigorous criticism; for example, by O'Higgins (1980), Tanzi (1982), and Bank of England (1982). There appears to be little evidence for Freud's assertion that 'people tend to pay their "black" plumbing bills for, say, £100 in £10 and £20 notes, rather than in £1 or £5 notes' (Freud, 1979). Large drug transactions and other activities in organised crime may indeed be, at least in part, settled using large notes. But, as Tanzi (1982) observes, many black economy payments (of baby-sitters, window-cleaners, and so on) are generally settled using the smaller denominations that most people use for everyday transactions in the formal economy too.

But the most serious criticism of the 'large bills method' is what O'Higgins terms the 'substitution effect' of inflation on currency holdings. The value of large notes in circulation will tend to have to rise by more than the rate of inflation, quite apart from any growth in black economy activity using large bills. If the proportion of high-value notes in circulation were not to rise during a period of inflation, the *number* of notes would have to increase at the same pace as the rate of inflation. But this is unlikely. People have only so much space in their wallets, and as prices rise will tend to use fewer low-denomination notes and more high-denomination notes.

To illustrate the substitution effect in another way, consider, for example, a period during which, as a result of general inflation, prices double. It is reasonable to suppose that at the end of the period the number of £10 notes in use by the public will be the same as the number of £5 notes at the start of the period. The average denomination of notes would then have risen, at the rate of inflation, while the number of notes in circulation would have remained the same.

In fact, over the past ten years the average denomination of notes has risen by even less than this argument would suggest, and has failed to keep pace with the rate of inflation. The average denomination of notes in circulation in the UK rose by 120 per cent between 1972 and 1982, while retail prices rose by 290 per cent (Bank of England, 1982, p. 523). In real terms, therefore, the average denomination of notes in circulation in the UK has declined by 40 per cent over the ten-year period. The 'large notes method' thus provides no evidence of a growing black economy in the UK.

Ratio of cash to bank deposits

Gutmann (1977) based his widely quoted estimates of the size of the black economy in the US on the relationship between cash in circulation and demand deposits (non-interest-bearing deposits in banks, corresponding roughly to current accounts in the UK). Since 1961 the ratio of cost to demand deposits had been rising in the US, as the value of currency in circulation rose faster than the aggregate value of demand deposits. Gutmann contrasted this trend with the pattern of financial innovation which has tended to encourage a decline in the use of cash, in favour of cheques and other methods of payment. As Tanzi (1982) remarks, 'A modern economy is supposed to move out of currency, not into it'.

Gutmann attributed the rise in the ratio of cash to demand deposits to growth in the black economy. Basing his work on the assumption that no black economy existed during the period 1937–41 (when the ratio of cash to demand deposits was at its lowest point) Gutmann concluded that the black economy in the

US in 1976 amounted to $176 billion, equivalent to about 10 per cent of the nation's reported gross national product.

Gutmann's method has been widely criticised. In particular the implicit assumption that changes in the cash:demand deposits ratio are a reflection principally of changes in the demand for cash has been disputed. It appears, in fact, that much of the growth in the US cash:demand deposits ratio has resulted from slow growth in demand deposits rather than unusually rapid growth in the demand for cash. Financial innovation has meant that some money formerly held as demand deposits has been switched to other kinds of account, leading to the observed decline in the cash:demand deposits ratio.

In any event, if applied to the UK, Gutmann's method does not support the hypothesis of a growing black economy in the UK. As Figure 10.2 shows, the ratio of cash to UK private sector sight deposits remained steady throughout the 1960s and 1970s, and appears to have declined sharply since the start of the 1980s. Gutmann's method would therefore imply no change in the UK black economy during the 1960s and 1970s, and a decline in the level of underground activity during the 1980s.

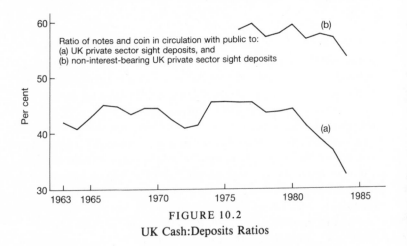

FIGURE 10.2

UK Cash:Deposits Ratios

The ratio shown as (a) in Figure 10.2 does not, in fact, correspond precisely to that used by Gutmann. The concept of private sector sight deposits is a broader one than that of the non-interest-bearing demand deposits that appear in the denominator of Gutmann's ratio. UK sight deposits contain some interest-bearing accounts (about 22 per cent of total sight deposits in 1980), and separate data for these have only been available since September 1975. A second ratio using non-interest-bearing sight deposits as denominator is shown as (b) in Figure 10.2, for the years for which data are available. This ratio has declined by much less since the start of the 1980s than the ratio of (a) has, implying that the fall observed in (a) has largely reflected substitution between interest-bearing sight deposits and other assets, rather than any change in the use of cash at all.

Gutmann's method, which shows a growing black economy in the US, would appear to point to a declining black economy in the UK. Perhaps this is so. But it is really quite difficult to believe that the method in fact sheds much light on the scale of the black economy in either country. The cash:deposits ratio is affected by too many other variables to be of much use as an indicator of cash use in the black economy.

'Causal' methods

A more sophisticated approach to measuring the scale of the black economy from cash data is exhibited by the 'causal' models of Tanzi (1980), Matthews (1983), and Matthews and Rastogi (1985). These attempt to explain the growth of currency holdings in terms of factors thought likely to have an influence on the size of the black economy. Thus, rather than attributing to the black economy every change in the demand for cash, or all changes that cannot be explained in terms of a limited number of conventional variables, this method follows a more cautious approach. It attributes to the black economy only those parts of changes in cash demand that can be statistically related to changes in the supposed determinants of the black economy, and leaves open the possibility that cash demand might also have been affected by other, unknown factors, statistical errors, etc.

Tanzi (1980) working with US data and Matthews (1983) with UK data have both attempted to explain changes in the ratio of cash to a broader monetary aggregate. To this extent, these studies are a natural progression from Gutmann's work on the cash:deposits ratio, although in each case the denominator chosen is somewhat wider than the value of non-interest-bearing deposits used by Gutmann. Tanzi's denominator is M2 (the sum of currency, demand deposits, and time deposits), while Matthews uses the sum of current and deposit accounts in his ratio.

The method used is an extension of that of Cagan (1958). The ratio of cash to bank deposits is explained in terms of the factors likely to affect the ratio in the absence of the black economy, together with further factors which the authors suggest may have contributed to growth in the black economy. Their argument is that, to the extent that these factors have led to a higher level of activity in the black economy, they will have increased demand for currency relative to bank deposits.

Thus the ratio of the total amount of cash in circulation to the level of bank deposits is a function of the level of transactions in the formal economy and in the black economy, and of the opportunity cost of holding cash:

$$C/D = f(Y_F, Y_B, r) \tag{1}$$

where C/D is the cash:deposits ratio, Y_F is a measure of the total value of transactions in the formal economy, Y_B is the total value of transactions in the black economy, and r is the rate of interest that could otherwise have been earned by depositing the cash in an interest-bearing account. The cash:deposits ratio is expected to be positively related to both transactions in the formal economy and transactions in the black economy (in other words, more transactions require more cash), and negatively related to the rate of interest (in other words, the higher the rate of interest that could be earned by depositing the cash in an interest-bearing account, the more people will economise on their use of cash).

The level of transactions in the black economy, while it cannot be observed, is believed to be affected by a number of factors, perhaps including tax and social security benefit levels (providing the incentive to work in the black economy), and the risks and penalties resulting from detection. While the risks and penalties associated with detection may be partly subjective, and in any case difficult to measure, the incentives provided by tax and benefit levels can be quantified. Amongst other factors, therefore, the level of transactions in the black economy will be a function of tax and benefit rates:

$$Y_B = g(t, B) \tag{2}$$

where t represents one or more tax rates, and B the level of unemployment benefit in real terms.

Substituting (2) into (1) gives an equation for the ratio of cash to deposits, as a function of, amongst other things, transactions in the formal economy, the rate of interest, tax rates and benefit levels:

$$C/D = h(Y_F, r, t, B)$$

Tanzi and Matthews both estimate equations of this form, although their final estimating equations include a lagged value of the dependent variable on the right-hand side, reflecting a view that cash holdings adjust only slowly to changes in the levels of transactions, the rate of interest, etc.

The currency:deposit ratio equation estimated by Matthews (1983) for the UK used quarterly observations for a sample period from the third quarter of 1971 to the end of 1980. The final equation he estimated included three possible determinants of the size of the black economy: t_y which is a measure of the average income tax rate (including National Insurance contributions) paid by a married man with two children, t_e which is the rate of the employer's National Insurance contribution, and B which is an estimate of the level of unemployment benefit and other allowances in real terms. Various lagged values of these variables were used; it is unclear whether alternative lag structures were tested, and on what basis the particular lagged values used were chosen. Neither the average income tax rate nor the level of real benefits is statistically significant at the 5 per cent level on a two-tailed test (i.e. there is a more than 5 per cent probability that the apparent relationship between the cash:deposits ratio and these variables could have occurred simply as the result of chance). While the rate of the employer's National Insurance contribution does appear to be significantly related to the cash:deposit ratio, the second period lagged value has the 'wrong' (i.e. negative) sign. Overall, the equation exhibits substantial autocorrelation.

Nevertheless, despite the fact that the equation is unsatisfactory in these respects, Matthews appears to use this equation (including the variables that are not statistically significant) to estimate the size of the UK's black economy. He estimates that this fell from 5.5 per cent of UK recorded GDP in 1972 to 2.3 per cent in 1974, and then rose to 7.0 per cent of GDP in 1978, 12.1 per cent in 1980 and 15.9 per cent in 1983. (This last figure is based on the 'Liverpool forecast of GDP and post-sample prediction of the currency:deposit ratio', rather than measured values.) Using these estimates of the black economy, and the wage and unemployment equations in the 'Liverpool model', Matthews makes some illustrative estimates of what these figures imply for the true level of unemployment. He estimates that the number of registered unemployed who were actually employed in the black economy could have risen from 122,000 in 1972 to 525,000 in 1980 and 1,290,000 in 1983. He concludes that 'if our estimates of the black economy are anything to go by, it is likely that a sizeable proportion of unemployment generated in the latter half of the decade [the 1970s] represents a monumental statistical illusion' (Matthews, 1983, p. 266).

In a more recent paper Matthews has returned to the relationship between cash demand and the black economy. Matthews and Rastogi (1985) look at the demand for currency in real terms, rather than the currency:deposits ratio, and use annual data for the period 1957–83. By switching attention to the real demand for currency, they avoid the problem already noted with the cash:deposits ratio, which is that variation in the ratio may be due as much to variation in the use of bank deposits as to variation in the use of cash. Other studies of the real demand for currency have been made by Johnston (1984), who did not explore the role of black economy variables, and the Bank of England (1982), which did, and which concluded that they had had no influence on the demand for notes and coin.

One of the equations estimated by Matthews and Rastogi is shown in Table 10.2; they also report an 'instrumental variables' estimate which, because of the lack of information about how it was estimated, is harder to evaluate. The definitions of the variables used are much the same as in the earlier paper except that the dependent variable is now the 'wide money base', M0, which is predominantly made up of notes and coin in circulation outside the Bank of England. (It includes, in addition to notes and coin in circulation with the public, banks' till money and banks' operational balances at the Bank of England.)

In this equation, none of the three 'black economy' variables are significant at the 5 per cent level on a two-tailed test, and in the instrumental variables estimate only the rate of employer's National Insurance contributions appears to be significant.

TABLE 10.2

Real Demand for Notes and Coin

(a) *Matthews and Rastogi*
   Dependent variable is log(real M0); sample 1957–83 (27 observations)

	Constant	R_{t-1}	$\log\{GDP(1-t_y)\}$	$\log(M0/P)_{t-1}$	t_y	t_e	$\log B$	$\bar{R}^2$
	-2.463	-0.660	0.565	0.622	0.304	0.178	0.120	0.9837
	(1.39)	(1.48)	(2.76)	(6.38)	(1.47)	(1.53)	(1.83)	

(b) *Corresponding estimates, notes and coin equation*
   Dependent variable is log(real notes and coin); sample 1958–83 (26 observations)

	Constant	R_{t-1}	$\log PDI$	$\log(NC/P)_{t-1}$	t_y	t_e	$\log B$	$\bar{R}^2$
	0.260	-0.014	0.050	0.731	-0.002	0.001	0.286	0.9325
	(0.32)	(5.42)	(0.64)	(9.26)	(0.99)	(0.67)	(0.96)	

Notes: t-values are shown in parentheses below the coefficients.
            Definitions of variables are given in the text.

Nevertheless, the estimated coefficients of all three 'black economy' variables in the instrumental variables equation are again used to estimate the growth of the black economy. This time it is assumed that the black economy was of negligible size in 1960, and it is estimated to have grown rapidly to 12.8 per cent of GDP by 1970, and continued to remain broadly steady at around 14 per cent until 1983, when it was 14.5 per cent of GDP.

Again, it will be observed that the estimates are based on regression coefficients some of which are not statistically significant at the 5 per cent level. In addition, our re-estimation of Matthews's and Rastogi's equation using slightly different data suggests that the results are, at the very least, rather sensitive to the precise form of the equation estimated.

The second equation in Table 10.2 is our re-estimation of Matthews's and Rastogi's equation using similar, but not completely identical, data. The three 'black economy' variables used are the same ones that Matthews and Rastogi used (and, indeed, are copied from the graphs in their paper), but the dependent variable, the rate of interest, and the measure of activity in the formal economy differ slightly. The dependent variable is the real value of notes and coin in circulation with the public (rather than real M0), the rate of interest is the rate on banks' deposit accounts (rather than the Treasury bill rate), and formal economy activity is measured by real personal disposable income (rather than Matthews's and Rastogi's variable which is based on GDP at factor cost reduced by the amount of their income tax variable t''). Each of these three modifications in our view represents an improvement on the Matthews and Rastogi variables, given the particular issue (of the amount of notes and coin held by the public for their transactions in the black economy) that is at stake. The estimated equation has a lot of similarities with theirs; again the three 'black economy' variables are not significant at the 5 per cent level, although in this equation the income tax variable is perversely signed. The following features of this estimated equation can be observed.

Firstly, not only are the three 'black economy' variables not statistically significant in our equation, but also there appears to be a strong case for leaving them out of the equation altogether. Table 10.3 shows that leaving all three 'black economy' variables out of

TABLE 10.3

Real Demand for Notes and Coin: The 'Black Economy' Variables

Dependent variable is log(real notes and coin), sample 1958–83 (26 observations)

	Constant	R_{t-1}	log PDI	$\log(NC/P)_{t-1}$	t_y	t_e	log B	$\bar{R}^2$	F
Eqn 1	0.260 (0.32)	-0.014 (5.42)	0.050 (0.64)	0.731 (9.26)	-0.002 (0.99)	0.001 (0.67)	0.286 (0.96)	0.932	58.5
Eqn 2	0.188 (0.24)	-0.014 (5.45)	0.055 (0.72)	0.734 (9.45)	-0.002 (0.94)		0.291 (0.99)	0.934	72.1
Eqn 3	0.568 (0.77)	-0.015 (6.41)	0.033 (0.43)	0.735 (9.53)		0.001 (0.56)	0.157 (0.59)	0.933	70.1
Eqn 4	0.488 (0.68)	-0.015 (6.54)	0.038 (0.52)	0.737 (9.52)			0.169 (0.64)	0.935	90.5
Eqn 5	0.124 (0.29)	-0.015 (7.41)	0.081 (2.67)	0.765 (12.00)				0.936	123.8

Notes: t-values are given in parentheses below the coefficients; critical value for 5 per cent significance on two-tailed test = 2.09 in equation 1.

Definitions of variables are given in the text.

the equation appears to improve its overall significance, and the significance of the remaining variables.

Secondly, the only one of the three 'black economy' variables to have much quantitative 'leverage' on real cash demand is the benefit rate. The product of the coefficient on $\log B$ and the standard deviation of $\log B$ over the period is 0.126, while the product of the coefficient of t_y and its standard deviation is 0.012, and of t_e and its standard deviation is 0.004. In other words, if we were to use this equation to estimate the time-profile of the black economy, the profile would be largely related to the profile of real benefit levels. It is not possible to make a similar estimate of the 'contribution' of each 'black economy' variable to the size of the black economy estimated by Matthews and Rastogi, since they give no information about the 'scaling' of their variables. Without this information it is not possible to infer anything from the coefficients in the equations they publish.

Thirdly, suppose that the coefficients in the second equation in Table 10.2 were significant, and that it therefore could be legitimate to try to estimate the size of the black economy from the equation. The size of the black economy would rise sharply during the 1960s and remain broadly steady throughout the 1970s (much as Matthews's and Rastogi's figures do, in fact). But the time-profile of actual unemployment has a very different pattern, rising only slowly during the 1960s, from about 360,000 in 1960 to about 610,000 in 1970, and then rising to 1.4 million in 1979 and nearly 3 million in 1983. It would therefore appear that the black economy had expanded most at a time when unemployment rose by comparatively little. Thus, despite the fact that real benefit levels are quantitatively the most important of the three black economy variables in the estimated equation, these results give little reason to believe that the black economy is a phenomenon closely related to the rise in unemployment.

Transactions approach

Finally, although it is not, strictly speaking, a cash-based measurement approach, brief mention should be made here of the 'transactions approach' developed by Feige. This approach, applied initially to the US in Feige (1979) and Feige (1980), and subsequently to the UK in Feige (1981), has been responsible for some extremely high estimates of the size of the black economy.

Feige (1981), for example, concludes that the UK's 'monetary unobserved sector' (which appears to correspond to what we have called the black economy) grew sharply between 1960 and 1974, to a peak of some 23 per cent of GDP, but by 1975 had fallen back to around 15 per cent of GDP, and remained steady at this level for the remainder of the decade.

The method is based on what Feige (1981) describes as 'a simplifying assumption which has been employed by monetary economists for over fifty years'—namely, 'that there exists a relatively stable relationship between the *volume* of non-financial transactions and the *income* produced by them'. The method uses the Fisher identity:

$$MV \equiv PT$$

where M is the stock of money, V its velocity of circulation, P the price level, and T the total volume of transactions.

Essentially, what Feige tries to do is to calculate an independent estimate of income based on an estimate of the level of transactions derived from this equation, and then to compare this estimate of income with official income statistics. The main problem in using the Fisher equation to do this is that the velocity of circulation is difficult—if not impossible—to measure. Feige (1981) gives inadequate information about how he has measured velocity, but it would appear that his estimates are based on, amongst other things, his assessment of the number of times a pound note can change hands before physically disintegrating to the point where it is withdrawn from circulation.

The reader may feel that this is a little far-fetched, and Feige himself admits that the figures 'may be quite sensitive to alternative specifying assumptions and are likely to contain substantial measurement error'. It is a pity that Feige gives little information about his assumptions, and does not explore alternative assumptions in his paper. Certainly, without rigorous examination of Feige's assumptions, it is difficult to attach any credence to his results.

Conclusions

Attempts to infer the size of the black economy from the amount of cash in circulation have sometimes concluded that the UK black economy is very large. However, there are a number of reasons for believing that cash measurement methods shed very little light on the black economy. In the first place, these methods are based on an assumption that black economy transactions are generally made in cash; this assumption has never been adequately tested. Secondly, there have been massive changes in the pattern of cash use in the past decade, due to rapid financial innovation. These changes are likely to make it extremely difficult to discern any effect of the black economy on cash demand. Thirdly, although a wide range of cash indicators of the black economy have been suggested, few are at all plausible, and they tend to give widely varying results. Estimates of the size of the black economy based on cash indicators are best ignored.

Chapter 11

Evidence from national accounts discrepancies

Gross domestic product can, in principle, be calculated in three different ways. The 'expenditure' method adds up all final expenditures on goods and services by individuals, companies, and the government, and the net final expenditure of the overseas sector. The 'income' method adds up the total of factor incomes (i.e. incomes earned from the production of goods and services). The 'output' method adds up the output of various industries in the economy. In theory, so long as a consistent set of prices is used for valuation throughout, the three estimates of gross domestic product (GDP) should be the same. Total expenditures on goods and services (counting stockbuilding as an expenditure) should equal the total output of goods and services. Total expenditures on both consumption and investment goods and services should be identically equal to the factor incomes earned from producing and selling those goods and services. Hence in theory the three measures of GDP should be exactly equal, i.e.

$$GDP(E) = GDP(I) = GDP(O)$$

where E, I, and O refer to the expenditure, income, and output methods of estimating GDP respectively.

In practice, the three different ways of calculating GDP do not give exactly the same answer. Each of the three is an estimate, based on only partial information about expenditures, incomes, and outputs in the whole economy; all are based on information about samples taken from the whole economy, rather than a complete enumeration of all economic activity. While, in general, estimation based on a sample of economic activity is likely to be a reasonable guide to the level of GDP, it is unlikely ever to be exact. For statistical reasons, therefore, there are likely to be differences between GDP(E), GDP(I), and GDP(O).

Errors are also likely to be introduced into the estimates of GDP if economic activity is deliberately concealed from the authorities. Firms conducting a certain proportion of their business 'off-the-books' to evade value added tax (VAT) and profits tax will declare less than their true turn-over to the revenue authorities. They may also declare less than their true turn-over to any statistical inquiry, for fear that the two different arms of 'officialdom' may 'swap notes' and uncover the deception. If the output estimate of GDP were based on the statistical survey or on the turn-over declared to the revenue authorities, then the off-the-books business would not be included in the estimate of GDP(O). Similarly, if the estimate of GDP(I) were based on incomes declared for income tax purposes, then it would not reflect incomes that were concealed to avoid tax.

The possibility exists that the income, expenditure, and output measures of GDP may be affected differently by the concealment of economic activity in the black economy. The discrepancy between different estimates of GDP might then provide an indication of the extent of the black economy. This approach was used by MacAfee (1980) in his work on the hidden economy and the UK national accounts. MacAfee argued that the income- and expenditure-based measures of gross domestic product at current prices 'result from two almost wholly independent methods of estimation':

> The estimates of the expenditure measure of GDP are derived mainly from a wide range of industrial and household surveys designed specifically for statistical purposes and from central government and local authority accounting data.... It is believed that estimates of items of final expenditure are unbiased since there is little reason for respondents to the Family Expenditure Survey or other enquiries to disguise or exaggerate expenditure except in the case of sensitive items of household expenditure such as alcoholic drink.
> (MacAfee, 1980, p. 81)

On the other hand the income-based measure of GDP is largely based on data collected through the Inland Revenue. Wages and salaries, by far the largest component of GDP(I), are calculated mainly from tax forms filled in by employers, with some addition for earnings below the tax threshold. Of the other components of GDP(I), income from self-employment is initially based on incomes reported to the Inland Revenue by the self-employed, and the gross trading profits of companies are mainly estimated from accounts submitted to the Inland Revenue by companies operating in the UK. To the extent that any of these tax returns attempt to hide some income from the Inland Revenue in order to evade tax, the income-based measure of GDP could be understated.

MacAfee observed that the initial estimates of the two measures of GDP made on the bases of income and of expenditure differed by between 1 and 4 per cent of GDP, with the income measure consistently lower than the expenditure measure. The gap between the two, referred to as the 'initial residual difference', averaged about 1 per cent of GDP during the 1960s, but it widened considerably during the period 1973 to 1978, to about $3\frac{1}{2}$ per cent of GDP. Assuming the errors of estimation to be random, MacAfee concluded that the trend line of the initial residual difference represented unreported income, amounting to perhaps $3\frac{1}{2}$ per cent of GDP in 1978.

The published figures for GDP(I) were adjusted upwards, to take account of the apparent under-reporting of incomes. This adjustment—the 'evasion adjustment'—was based largely on the trend of the initial residual difference. It had been increased since the 1960s, to about $2\frac{1}{2}$ per cent of GDP in 1978. The published income estimate of GDP in 1978 was thus lower than the expenditure estimate, but the remaining difference—the 'residual error'—was assumed to reflect random statistical factors rather than systematic income under-reporting.

The behaviour of the initial residual difference since MacAfee's work was done—and subsequent revisions to the statistics on which MacAfee's report was based—seem to confirm that part at least of the very high difference between GDP(E) and GDP(I) in the mid-1970s reflected transient statistical factors rather than income under-reporting. Figure 11.1 shows that the initial residual difference has declined sharply since the mid-1970s, to a level lower even than in the 1960s. In 1984, indeed, the initial residual difference was negative; in other words, the initial estimate of the income measure of GDP exceeded the initial estimate of the expenditure measure.

At the very least, these changes in the initial residual difference do not suggest a rising trend in tax evasion. The evasion adjustment made by the Central Statistical Office to the income measure of GDP has fallen considerably since the mid-1970s, from 3 per cent of GDP in 1976 to 1.25 per cent in 1984. At present, the negative

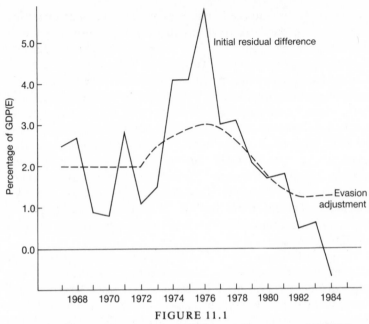

FIGURE 11.1
Initial Residual Difference and Evasion Adjustment to UK GDP

initial residual difference in 1984 is probably best explained in terms of the influence of random statistical factors, and maybe should not at this stage be taken as reflecting anything more than this. Clearly, though, a run of negative initial residual differences would begin to raise questions about the accuracy of the GDP(E) estimate, in much the same way as the basic positive residuals in the mid-1970s focused attention on possible under-recording of incomes.

The sharp rise and fall in the initial residual difference in the mid-1970s may be a reflection of a temporary rise in the level of income not declared for tax. It cannot be ruled out that the black economy may have grown sharply between 1974 and 1976, and declined just as much between 1976 and 1979. But such an interpretation of the initial residual difference stretches credulity a little, given the lack of obvious factors that could explain both the phenomenal growth and the precipitous decline of the black economy in such a short period. Over the period there were of course changes in the level of both tax rates and social security benefits, which might have influenced the development of the shadow economy, but the evidence of Chapters 5 and 8 certainly does not show a sharp rise in incentive to 'black' activity prior to 1974, reversed equally sharply by 1976.

Two other factors could have played a part in the high initial residual differences during the mid-1970s, although it is unlikely ever to be possible to determine how significant they in fact were. One possibility is that pay freezes may have tended to promote the growth of other forms of remuneration, such as payment-in-kind. It is possible that a change in the level of payment-in-kind might have been reflected in some part in expenditure statistics, but to a lesser extent in the estimates of income. On the other hand, if this were so, the course of the initial residual difference suggests, perhaps rather surprisingly, that the use of such ways round the pay policy fell quite strongly in the years between 1976 and 1979 while the policy was in operation. Moreover there appear to have been no corresponding discrepancies arising from any similar growth of non-financial remuneration during the earlier period of pay restraint under the Heath Government in 1970–4.

A second possible source of the widening initial residual difference during the mid-1970s may have been the rise in the inflation rate itself, which may have increased the importance of timing discrepancies between the data on which the two estimates of GDP are based. Clearly, when prices are rising at 20 per cent a year, it matters a lot at what time of the year the observations of expenditure are made, while when prices are rising slowly the timing of observations may be less crucial. Such an explanation might fit the pattern of the initial residual difference in the mid-1970s quite well, although it invites the question of why a corresponding divergence between the income and expenditure estimates of GDP did not accompany the acceleration of inflation in 1979.

What parts of the black economy are reflected in the discrepancy?

It was recognised by MacAfee, and deserves further emphasis, that the initial residual difference between GDP(E) and GDP(I) can at best give an indication of certain parts only of the black economy. The main aspect of the black economy that might give rise to a discrepancy between recorded expenditures and reported incomes is that involving the under-reporting of incomes for tax purposes. But, as already observed, the black economy involves a range of different phenomena in addition to income tax evasion.

Expenditures on illegal goods and services, and the corresponding factor incomes, may not be recorded, and neither GDP(E) nor GDP(I) will reflect such transactions. Some income-in-kind too may not be recorded, especially if those receiving it are uncertain about the legality of the arrangement. At the extreme this would encompass employee theft, about which the Family Expenditure Survey (FES) makes no enquiries. Intermediate cases include the incomes-in-kind of some waiters and other workers in the catering trade, documented by Mars and Nicod (1981), which appear, to some extent at least, to be condoned by employers and regarded as part of normal remuneration by some catering workers. The legal status of 'knock-off' food in the catering trade may nonetheless be sufficiently ambiguous for people to be extremely coy about it when reporting incomes-in-kind to FES interviewers, and both GDP(E) and GDP(I) may fail to reflect fully even legal incomes-in-kind.

The extent of off-the-books business by tradesmen—for example, by painters and decorators or other firms in the building industry—is unlikely to be fully indicated by the discrepancy between the income and expenditure estimates of GDP. Concealed incomes arising from off-the-books activity would of course be picked up by this method, but it would give no indication of the proportion of turn-over on which VAT was being evaded.

How 'working while claiming' and other social security frauds might affect the initial residual difference is even more difficult to assess. Much income from working while claiming is also likely to be concealed from the Inland Revenue (partly because of the risk of discovery through the correlation of National Insurance benefit and contribution records), but other income, while not reported, may in fact be reflected in the allowances made in the national accounts for incomes below the tax threshold.

For these reasons it is evident that there is no way of inferring the total amount of tax evaded (nor yet still of benefit fraud) from the discrepancy between GDP(E) and GDP(I), nor even that the discrepancy would prove an adequate guide to the total factor incomes earned in the black economy.

Data sources and the interpretation of the initial residual difference

The use of the initial residual difference between GDP(E) and GDP(I) as an indicator of the extent of the black economy depends on two crucial assumptions: first, that the two estimates of GDP are produced independently of each other; second, that even if the income measure of GDP is affected by evasion, the expenditure measure of GDP is a broadly accurate reflection of the overall level of expenditure in the economy. There are, in fact, grounds for scepticism on both counts. The two measures of GDP are not estimated entirely independently; more importantly, perhaps, the methods used to estimate the expenditure measure of GDP rely on a range of data sources, some of which are likely to be less than comprehensive in their coverage of expenditures. The recent low levels of the initial residual difference should not therefore be allowed to encourage complacency about the accuracy of the GDP estimates in general or about their vulnerability to the growth of black economy activities in particular.

It would be unfair to suggest that MacAfee was unaware of this. He explicitly notes that in some places the methods actually employed to estimate GDP(E) sometimes differ from the somewhat idealised account he had outlined earlier: 'For more accurate and timely figures inquiries to retailers and others are used for certain items. However, by switching the enquiry point to the vendor rather than the buyer it is possible that the sale of goods by informal producers will be missed'. As an example, he suggests that the informal sale of home-made wines to friends and neighbours will be missed since expenditure on alcohol is estimated by using Customs and Excise statistics on quantities on which duties have been paid.

But far from being exceptional, the use of data from sources other than expenditure surveys to estimate components of GDP(E) appears to be quite extensive. The Central Statistical Office (CSO) 'Blue Book' contains detailed estimates of consumers' expenditure, classified under sixty-five separate headings. Expenditure on only about a quarter of the items included under consumers' expenditure is estimated from sample surveys of consumers' expenditure (mainly the National Food Survey and the Family Expenditure Survey), and a variety of other sources are used for the remainder. Most of the remainder is, in fact, estimated from

STAFFORDSHIRE POLYTECHNIC LIBRARY

statistics of retail sales or turn-over, building up a picture of consumers' expenditure as seen from the 'other side of the counter'.

For many purposes the use of retail sales figures rather than expenditure survey data to estimate consumers' expenditure has considerable advantages. Not least among the virtues of this method is its timeliness. Preliminary indications of trends in consumers' expenditure can be derived from statistics of sales of a relatively small number of large retailers, and can be available considerably sooner than a similar statistical coverage of consumers.

In addition, surveys of consumers' expenditure are frequently felt to be unreliable, particularly with regard to spending on certain items, and tend to have a fairly low response rate. The FES, for example, appears to understate quite considerably consumers' expenditure on alcohol and tobacco (either because respondents under-report their drinking and smoking, or because alcoholics and heavy smokers do not fill in questionnaires), and its estimates of spending on certain 'lumpy' items (cars, washing machines, expensive holidays, and home improvements, for example) tend to be based on a relatively small number of respondents reporting expenditure during the weeks in question, and thus have a high risk of error. In addition, it is known that the FES respondents are not entirely representative of the population as a whole; a lower proportion of high-income earners and residents of the south of the country reply to the FES. Also the FES does not sample any of the population living in institutions.

Nevertheless for other purposes there may be drawbacks to using sales data to estimate consumers' expenditure. Consider, for example, the case of a small painting and decorating firm, conducting a certain proportion of its business off-the-books, both to evade liability for VAT on that proportion of its business and to allow it to employ a number of workers on a cash basis, making a saving on tax and National Insurance costs. Since there is nothing illegal in paying cash for painting and decorating, it is quite likely that household spending on the off-the-books activity would be reported to the Family Expenditure Survey. On the other hand it is much less likely that the firm itself would report the off-the-books activity to a government survey, even if confidentiality were guaranteed.

MacAfee's attempt to estimate the scale of the black economy by comparing the income and expenditure measures of GDP would, on the face of it, appear to be largely vitiated by the use of sales data to estimate consumers' expenditure. A growing black economy involving both income tax evasion and off-the-books business would lead to both the income and the expenditure measures of GDP being understated; the difference between the two would simply be an indication of which had been understated by more. On this interpretation, of course, a zero or negative initial residual difference could easily be compatible with a high level of black economy activity.

This is, however, perhaps an unduly stark account of the implications of using sales rather than expenditure data to estimate GDP(E). Over the longer term, the estimation method used may tend to lead to more accurate GDP(E) estimates than pure reliance on sales data would imply. Many of the sources of sales data are in fact incomplete, some being surveys only of larger retailers, for example. Assumptions then have to be made about how the data from these surveys are to be scaled up to reflect sales by all retailers. This 'bench-marking' process may in practice draw on a number of sources of supplementary information, including estimates of aggregate expenditures from the FES, to estimate the appropriate scaling factor for the retail sales data. At the point of bench-marking, the retail sales data would be as accurate as data from an expenditure survey, and problems would only arise subsequently if black economy sales had grown at a different rate from the survey sales since the bench-marking. Moreover where this had happened, subsequent matching with expenditure survey estimates would indicate any growing under-recording in the GDP(E) estimates.

Consumers' expenditure: Blue Book and the FES compared

While the Family Expenditure Survey and the National Food Survey are used for only about a quarter of the items of consumers' expenditure in the Blue Book, there is no reason, in principle at least, that all the items of consumers' expenditure could not be estimated from existing expenditure survey data. The FES provides sufficient detail and sufficient coverage to make alternative expenditure estimates for all the items of consumers' expenditure in the Blue Book, at present up to and including 1983. Such estimates would not, of course, be as timely as the published estimates; nor could the method be used to make reliable quarterly estimates. But for the purposes of estimating the extent of the black economy from a comparison of GDP(E) and GDP(I), an estimate of GDP(E) based on FES consumers' expenditure data would appear to have some advantages over the existing, published, GDP(E) estimates.

There are, it should be observed, some conceptual differences between the Family Expenditure Survey and the national accounts estimates of consumers' expenditure. The FES surveys the expenditure of households resident in the United Kingdom, and does not include the expenditures by

- people living in institutions such as prisons and hospitals,
- private non-profit-making bodies serving persons,
- foreign tourists in the UK, or
- children under the age of sixteen.

The Blue Book figures for consumers' expenditure, by contrast, include these expenditures. Spending by people living in institutions and by children under sixteen is included throughout; spending by foreign tourists in the UK is included in the individual expenditure items, but subtracted from the overall total of consumers' expenditure; spending by private non-profit-making bodies is not included in the individual expenditure items, but is added in to the total of consumers' expenditure.

The process of moving from the FES data on average household expenditure on individual goods and services to a 'genuine expenditure' estimate of GDP(E) would require estimates to be made of spending by people living in institutions, children under sixteen, and private non-profit-making bodies serving persons. But none of these estimates appear to be all that large in relation to total spending, and so the errors introduced into the overall estimate of GDP(E) by inaccuracies in estimating these items are likely to be comparatively unimportant. A far more critical problem, which could have a significant effect on the estimate of GDP(E), is the appropriate scaling up of the FES sample of about 7,000 households (containing about 20,000 individuals) to the population as a whole.

Scaling up could be done in proportion to the number of individuals in the FES relative to the population as a whole, or in proportion to the number of households, or the number of tax units. The choice between these methods depends partly on whether satisfactory figures can be obtained for the total number of households or tax units in the population. Whilst rather arbitrary, the choice made may nonetheless be significant, as Atkinson and Micklewright (1982) have observed. For example, in 1972/3 grossing-up factors based on tax units were 5 per cent higher than those obtained from an individual basis.

Scaling up is complicated by the fact that the households included in the FES are known not to be entirely representative of the population as a whole. Households of some types tend to be less inclined to respond to the FES than others. A comparison of the FES with the 1971 Census of Population found that households with children and those where the head of the household was self-employed tended to have lower-than-average response rates, and there was a pronounced decline in response with increasing age. Partly for these reasons, higher-income households are thought to be under-represented in the FES results. It is probable therefore that the average expenditure of households that reply to the FES will be somewhat lower than the 'true' average expenditure for all households.

Ideally, the scaling-up factors used to move from the FES sample to the population as a whole should take account of these biases in the response to the survey. But in practice there are considerable difficulties. The variables that 'explain' non-response may be interrelated, and so it may not be adequate to scale up for each non-response factor separately. In addition, the appropriate scaling up may differ from product to product. Expenditures on private air travel, for example, are likely to be much more income-sensitive than expenditures on bus and coach travel, and would therefore tend to be more affected by the under-representation of high-income households in the FES. Recognising the complexity of an exact scaling up, we have chosen instead merely to scale up on the basis of the number of individuals in the FES and in the population as a whole, and to make no allowance for differential non-response. This means that the total is probably somewhat understated because of the lower representation of high-income earners (although understatement in the total from this source is unlikely to be large, probably amounting to only 2 or 3 per cent at most). The expenditure pattern is likely to be biased towards goods that form a greater proportion of the spending of lower-income consumers, and understatement in spending on individual items for which demand is highly income-elastic (e.g. air travel) could be considerable.

Table 11.1 shows the scaling-up factors used to move from household expenditure in the FES to total expenditure by the population as a whole. They are based on the number of individuals in the FES sample and the number of individuals in the population as a whole, subtracting 200,000 to reflect people living in hospitals, prisons, or other institutions where they incur negligible expenditures. This allowance is probably on the low side; a further 500,000 pensioners living in institutions could also have been subtracted (making a difference of about 1 per cent to the estimate of total expenditure), though in the absence of any survey data on the expenditure of the institutional population, treatment of expenditures by the institutional population is inevitably rather arbitrary.

The surprising outcome from scaling up Family Expenditure Survey data to make an alternative estimate of consumers' expenditure is shown in Table 11.2. Contrary to what might have

TABLE 11.1

Scaling-Up Factors for FES Data

	UK population (thousands)	FES SAMPLE Individuals	FES SAMPLE Households	Scaling-up factor[a]
	A	B	C	D
1979	56,227	18,314	6,777	1,081
1980	56,314	18,844	6,944	1,078
1981	56,379	20,535	7,525	1,073
1982	56,335	20,022	7,428	1,086
1983	56,377	18,532	6,973	1,102

[a] Scaling-up factor, D, calculated according to the formula:

$$D = \frac{(A - 200)}{1000} \times \frac{C}{B} \times \frac{365}{7}$$

Source: UK population: *Monthly Digest of Statistics*, April 1985, Table 2.1, mid-year estimate of de-facto or home population. *Family Expenditure Survey*, annual reports.

TABLE 11.2

Consumers' Expenditure: FES and Blue Book Estimates, £ million

	TOTAL CONSUMERS' EXPENDITURE			CONSUMERS' EXPENDITURE EXCLUDING ALCOHOL AND TOBACCO		
	FES	Blue Book	Ratio	FES	Blue Book	Ratio
1979	100,046	117,912	0.85	92,034	105,017	0.88
1980	117,786	136,789	0.86	108,450	122,013	0.89
1981	132,654	152,125	0.87	122,145	135,457	0.90
1982	142,857	166,538	0.86	132,017	148,649	0.89
1983	155,130	182,420	0.85	142,876	162,840	0.88

been expected from the earlier argument about the use of sales data to estimate consumers' expenditure, the estimates of consumers' expenditure based on the FES are significantly *lower* than the Blue Book figures. While the Blue Book estimates of consumers' expenditure might have been expected to have omitted expenditures on off-the-books black economy activity, they are in total higher by about 15 per cent than the estimates based on expenditure data from the Family Expenditure Survey, which might have been expected to include such expenditures.

Part of the discrepancy can be accounted for. Respondents to the Family Expenditure Survey appear to understate their spending on alcohol and tobacco quite considerably. Comparison with the Blue Book figures, which are based mainly on excise duty statistics and which are generally thought to be reasonably reliable, suggests that FES respondents report only about two-thirds of their actual spending on alcohol and tobacco. Excluding these items from the comparison of FES and Blue Book estimates of consumers' expenditure narrows the gap somewhat, to little more than 10 per cent.

Further understatement, though it is not clear how much, will arise from the response biases in the FES, especially the low representation of high-income households noted earlier. But re-weighting the data to increase the proportion of higher-income households would be unlikely to be sufficient to eliminate all the remaining gap; as already noted it is more likely to add 2 or 3 per cent to the expenditure total, rather than ten.

We are thus left with a considerable unexplained short-fall. It may in fact be the case that the Family Expenditure Survey under-records the level of expenditure, possibly because respondents are less diligent about filling in their spending diaries towards the end of the two-week survey period. (There is some internal evidence for this view: recorded spending is on average lower in the second week of the survey period than in the first week.) If this is so, then the hope that the FES could be used to make an estimate of GDP(E) that reflected black economy activities more fully than the Blue Book estimate, and that hence could be used to make a more accurate estimate of the discrepancy between the income and expenditure estimates of GDP, has been largely frustrated.

However, the estimates of consumers' expenditure based on the Family Expenditure Survey may nonetheless shed some light on the pattern, if not the level, of black economy activity. If the main reason that the aggregate estimate of consumers' expenditure based on the FES is too low is that respondents gradually become lazy about filling in the FES spending diaries, then it might not be unreasonable to assume that the understatement from this source would affect all expenditure items equally. On the other hand, all the anecdotal evidence points to the black economy being concentrated in certain expenditure areas, most notably in services provided to households, such as painting and decorating, repairs and maintenance, private tuition, window-cleaning, taxis, hairdressing, and so on. There are also, as we saw in Chapter 6, plausible theoretical arguments why the black economy should be most prominent in these areas. Other things being equal, we would expect that if 'black' activity were a large proportion of total activity in these areas, then this would be reflected in the ratio of Blue Book to FES-based estimates of items of consumers' expenditure at a disaggregated level. The products where the FES-based estimates of spending were high in relation to the Blue Book estimates would tend to be those where spending on off-the-books output failed to be recorded by the sales data used in making the Blue Book estimates.

Table 11.3 shows a comparison of FES and Blue Book estimates for items of consumers' expenditure. The FES data have been scaled using the factors in Table 11.1, and are shown as a percentage of the corresponding Blue Book estimate. In most of the cases where FES data (or, in the case of food, National Food Survey data) have been used as the basis for the Blue Book estimate, the two estimates are in broad agreement. Such differences as arise in these cases are probably due to the use of smoothed FES data for the Blue Book estimates, while unsmoothed data have been used in this comparison.

There is considerably greater variation in the items for which the FES is not used as the primary source for the Blue Book estimates. No doubt this partly reflects the judgement of the compilers of the national accounts that FES data are not an accurate reflection of consumers' expenditure on these products, and that a more accurate assessment can be made from other sources. Such a view may well be reasonable in the case, for example, of air travel, where the under-representation of high-income households in the FES may present particular problems and may largely account for the low estimate of spending on air travel from FES data. But underlying the variation, there appears to be a tendency for expenditure items where the Blue Book estimates are not based on the FES to be significantly under-estimated compared with those where the FES is the principal data source. For the five items where the FES was the primary data source, marked (1) in Table 11.3, the FES-based estimate was on average 93 per cent of the Blue Book figure, but for the fourteen items based on sales data marked (2) in Table 11.3, the FES-based estimate averaged only 87 per cent of the corresponding Blue Book figure. The difference is small and may not be significant. But it could imply that the scaling applied to FES data in the Blue Book might be a little low, and that spending on items such as household and domestic services, and hairdressing and beauty care could have been somewhat under-estimated in the Blue Book.

Apart from this, Table 11.3 shows little sign of the Blue Book consumers' expenditure being systematically under-estimated in cases where possible black economy expenditures might be important. Spending on the majority of the most frequently cited black economy goods and services is based in the Blue Book, at least in part, on FES data, and in those cases (e.g. house maintenance, catering) where the FES is used for only part of the estimate, basing the estimates on the FES throughout would be more likely to reduce, rather than to increase, the estimated expenditures.

TABLE 11.3

Comparison of FES and Blue Book Estimates for Items of Consumers' Expenditure

	FES estimate as percentage of Blue Book estimate, average 1979–83	Data source[a]
TOTAL CONSUMERS' EXPENDITURE	86	
FOOD	97	N
ALCOHOLIC DRINK	57	O
TOBACCO	72	O
CLOTHING AND FOOTWEAR	94	S (2)
HOUSING	95	
Rents, rates and water charges	95	O
Maintenance, etc. by occupiers	95	S/F
FUEL AND POWER	105	O
HOUSEHOLD GOODS AND SERVICES	90	
Furniture, pictures, etc.	77	S (2)
Carpets and other floor coverings	82	S (2)
Major appliances	102	S (2)
Textiles and soft furnishings	75	S (2)
Hardware	108	S (2)
Cleaning materials, matches	99	F (1)
Household and domestic services	93	F (1)

TRANSPORT AND COMMUNICATION	85		
Cars, motorcycles, and other vehicles	103	O	
Petrol and oil	96	O	
Vehicle excise duty	97	O	
Other running costs of vehicles	70	F/O	(1)
Rail travel	74	S	(2)
Buses and coaches	72	S	(2)
Air travel	20	O	
Other travel	98	O/F	
Posts and telecommunications	82	S	(2)
RECREATION, ENTERTAINMENT, AND EDUCATION	81		
Radio, TV, and other durable goods	105	S	(2)
TV and video rental, licence fees, etc.	96	S/F/O	
Sports goods, toys, games, camping equipment	65	S	(2)
Other recreational goods	82	S/F	
Betting and gaming	32	O	
Other recreational and entertainment services	78	O/F	
Books, newspapers, and magazines	99	F	(1)
Education	80	O	

TABLE 11.3 contd

Comparison of FES and Blue Book Estimates for Items of Consumers' Expenditure

	FES estimate as percentage of Blue Book estimate, average 1979–83	Data source[a]	
OTHER GOODS AND SERVICES	67	S	(2)
Pharmaceutical products and medical goods	89	S	(2)
NHS payments and other medical expenses	46	O/F	
Toilet articles, perfumery	91	S	(2)
Hairdressing and beauty care	102	F	(1)
Jewellery, silverware, watches, and clocks	63	S	
Other goods	103	S	(2)
Catering (meals and accommodation)	75	F/O	
Administration costs of life assurance and superannuation schemes	–		
Other services	59	O	
HOUSEHOLD EXPENDITURE ABROAD	79	O	

[a] N: National Food Survey;
S: retail sales data;
F: Family Expenditure Survey;
O: other.

Accuracy of the national accounts

We have seen that the Inland Revenue data used to estimate the income measure of gross domestic product understate the true level of income because of tax evasion, and that adjustments to the figures are made to compensate for this. We have also seen that, in principle at least, the majority of data sources used to estimate total expenditure would not measure expenditures in the black economy or off-the-books sales concealed by shops and other businesses. What reliance, therefore, can be placed on the GDP estimates included in the national accounts? Are they, despite these apparent loopholes in the estimation procedure, nonetheless an accurate measure of the nation's GDP? Or is it the case, as Feige (1981) and Matthews (1983) have argued, that the national accounts have failed to reflect growth in the black economy, and are now seriously in error?

The issue is by no means purely an academic one. Some writers have argued that the consequences of failing to take full account of black economy activities in measuring GDP and other macroeconomic statistics could be that serious mistakes could be made both in analysis of the present situation and in the policies adopted. For example Reuter (1982) suggests that 'Many issues in current macroeconomics which are treated as issues for theoretical resolution may well be the consequence of changes in the quality of the underlying data'. The fall in the growth rate in western economies since the early 1970s which has puzzled economists may, for example, be—at least in part—a statistical illusion, resulting from a failure to take into account in GDP statistics growth in the black economy.

Reuter (1982) argues that more attention should be paid to the possibility of error in economic statistics: 'Economists are unique among social scientists in that they are trained only to analyse, not to collect data ... One consequence is a lack of scepticism about the quality of data'. This means becoming more aware of the process by which statistics such as GDP are estimated: 'The data are not generated in some magical fashion by omniscient agencies; they are the result of reporting and monitoring programmes which are sensitive to changes in the structure of the economy' (Reuter, 1982).

It is, in fact, highly unlikely that the CSO's estimates of UK gross domestic product are now seriously in error because of changes in the black economy over the past two decades. There is no evidence to support the view that the black economy is now a substantial part of the nation's economic activity, or that it has grown sharply in recent years. The possibility of some—not inconsiderable—tax evasion is already included in the estimates; but even if actual tax evasion were twice the amount allowed, the error in the GDP estimates would be less than 2 per cent. (Tax evasion at this level would imply that about one-third of all self-employment income was not declared for tax, which must be close to the upper limit of the feasible amount of evasion.) Similarly, as Chapter 9 demonstrated, the percentage of total household expenditure that could be on goods and services from black economy producers is low—perhaps 2½ per cent. Again, some of these informal sales may already be reflected in the expenditure estimate of GDP, since consumer surveys are used as the primary data source for some expenditure items.

Nevertheless, while in practice the errors introduced into GDP by the black economy are likely to have been small, writers such as Gutmann, Feige, and Matthews have undoubtedly performed a useful service in drawing attention to the possibility of error from this source. It is useful to examine how vulnerable the GDP estimates could be to rapid black economy growth, and the extent to which the available cross-checks would be sufficient to identify growing errors resulting from the omission of black economy activities.

Cross-checking in the national accounts

The residual error between the income and expenditure estimates of GDP, which has been the subject of most of this chapter, is of course the main point at which a growing black economy should be identified. Increasing tax evasion should lead to progressive underestimation of incomes, while the level of expenditures, in so far as it is based on household survey data, should continue to be accurately recorded. In practice, as we have seen, the expenditure estimate is based less on expenditure survey data than on retail sales data and other data supplied by businesses. A growth in the share of sales taken by informal producers or other businesses not included in the survey, or a growing tendency for the businesses surveyed to conduct a proportion of their businesses off-the-books could lead to deterioration in the accuracy of the expenditure measure of GDP.

To some extent, a rise in the amount of business unrecorded in retail sales surveys could be identified from a growing gap between the alternative estimate of expenditure in the Family Expenditure Survey and the GDP estimate. A relatively high, but stable, level of unrecorded sales would be harder to identify since, as we have seen, there are considerable, unreconciled differences between the two sets of figures.

Inevitably, too, there will be a tendency for the gap between GDP(E) and GDP(I) to be minimised in the compilation of the statistics. At times when the initial residual difference is large and positive it is to be expected that resources will tend to be devoted to examining sources of possible understatement in the income measure; similarly if the initial residual difference is negative—as it is at present—efforts will tend to concentrate on identifying possible understatement in expenditures. While this is undoubtedly an appropriate pattern of response where the underlying structure of activity is known to be stable, it would tend to dampen the early warning signals of growing black economy activity.

The information that the initial residual difference gives about errors in the GDP estimates is limited; it generally does not help to pin-point the source of the errors. More disaggregated comparisons of the estimates, at the level of individual industries, can be helpful in identifying the source of a discrepancy. If the black economy is more extensive in certain industries than in others, greater discrepancies might be expected in those industries where the black economy was particularly large.

The income and expenditure data required for such a comparison at industry level are not published in the UK. However, a comparison is available between the expenditure and output measures of GDP at a disaggregated level in the 'commodity flow accounts' calculated by the CSO.

The commodity flow accounts and the black economy

The commodity flow accounts are a set of tables that match the supply and demand for some forty different commodity groups, covering the whole economy. They are a form of condensed input-output table, in that intermediate demand for each commodity is shown only in total, and not by individual purchasing industry. But they differ from the published UK input-output tables in that the discrepancies between supply and demand are shown explicitly, for each commodity.

The tables rest on an accounting identity between 'supply' (reflecting output) and 'demand' (reflecting expenditures and stockbuilding). The items included on each side of the identity are shown in Table 11.4.

TABLE 11.4

The Accounting Identity in Commodity Flow Accounts

Supply	Demand
Home output	Consumers' expenditure
Imports	Government expenditure
	Investment
	Stockbuilding
	Exports
	Intermediate demand

At an aggregate level the discrepancy between supply and demand (corresponding to the discrepancy between GDP(O) and GDP(E)) is small, averaging considerably less than 1 per cent in the six years 1978–83 (see Table 11.5). But the commodity flow accounts for each separate commodity group show a much larger discrepancy. In the thirty-nine accounts for marketed commodities shown in Table 11.6 the average absolute discrepancy in the annual figures was about 6 per cent.

The discrepancies may arise for a number of reasons quite unconnected with the black economy. The tables are shown in 'producer prices' (at factor cost) rather than market prices, and the conversion of expenditure data into producer prices may be in error. They are also shown in constant 1980 prices, and errors may be introduced in the process of deflation from current to constant prices. Other errors in estimation may also occur that have nothing to do with the black economy. But, granted all these other possible sources of error, how might a growing black economy affect the commodity flow accounts?

It is possible that a growing black economy would affect both

TABLE 11.5

Commodity Flow Account, Whole Economy (sum of 43 separate accounts),
producers' prices (at factor cost), £ million, 1980 prices, seasonally adjusted

	SUPPLY			DEMAND							DEMAND – SUPPLY	
	Home output	Imports	Total supply	Cons. exp.	GGFC	GDFCF	Stock-build.	Exports	Interm. demand	Total demand	D-S	$\frac{D-S}{S}$ (%)
1978	400,791	54,085	454,876	109,349	46,965	43,490	2,236	60,254	194,668	456,962	2,086	0.5
1979	410,592	59,822	470,414	114,264	47,996	44,759	2,493	62,629	197,917	470,058	-357	-0.1
1980	390,170	57,420	447,590	114,491	48,806	42,024	-3,517	62,524	184,249	448,578	988	0.2
1981	379,293	55,440	434,734	114,804	48,921	38,247	-2,910	61,565	176,886	437,513	2,780	0.6
1982	384,763	57,450	442,213	115,801	49,347	40,669	-865	62,314	178,367	445,633	3,420	0.8
1983	396,614	60,714	457,328	120,663	50,553	42,358	85	62,625	183,690	459,974	2,647	0.6

Source: CSO *Commodity Flow Accounts*, October 1984.

TABLE 11.6

Discrepancies in the Commodity Flow Accounts

	Percentage excess of demand over supply (average, 1978–83)
Agriculture, forestry, and fishing products	−0.2
Coal, coke, and other solid fuels	9.2
Mineral oil and natural gas	−3.1
Petroleum products	−8.0
Electricity	−3.5
Gas supply	−4.7
Water supply	−2.8
Minerals and ores	−6.7
Iron and steel	−6.0
Non-ferrous metals	14.7
Non-metallic mineral products	2.7
Chemicals and man-made fibres	2.9
Metal goods n.e.s.	6.2
Mechanical engineering products	4.0
Office machinery and data processing	5.7
Electrical engineering	−2.0
Motor vehicles (including parts)	12.6
Aerospace	−8.2
Ships and other vessels	10.4

Other vehicles	-1.7
Instrument engineering products	8.3
Manufactured food	2.1
Drink	5.3
Tobacco	2.3
Textiles	5.4
Clothing and footwear	15.2
Timber and furniture	8.9
Paper and board	6.4
Books	3.0
Rubber and plastics products	0.9
Other manufactured goods	-6.5
Construction	6.7
Distribution and repair	1.5
Hotels and catering	7.0
Rail transport	4.8
Other land transport	-11.5
Sea, air, and other transport	-5.2
Postal services and telecommunications	3.0
Miscellaneous services	-9.7

Source: CSO *Commodity Flow Accounts*, 1984.

sides of the identity. Consumers' expenditure within the commodity flow accounts is based on the data sources used to estimate consumers' expenditure in GDP. In a high proportion of industries, therefore, it is based on data from trade sources, and would not reflect growing off-the-books sales, or sales by informal suppliers. Home output is estimated mainly from the Annual Census of Production (ACOP), a survey conducted by the Business Statistics Office (BSO). The census excludes smaller firms, and is based on a register of firms (derived partly from VAT registrations) kept at the BSO. It is therefore unlikely to include the majority of business enterprises in the black economy—which, as we have argued, will be mainly smaller firms, often (legitimately or illegitimately) unregistered for VAT.

Once again, therefore, the usefulness of this information as a check on the accuracy of the data turns on the assumed accuracy of the consumers' expenditure estimates. If these are under-estimated, the commodity flow accounts may merely ensure consistency across the national accounts, without ensuring accuracy.

If, however, consumers' expenditure is correctly estimated (and, as we have seen, a comparison between Blue Book and FES-based consumers' expenditure estimates should at best make it possible to identify sharply increasing errors in the estimates), then the commodity flow accounts may be a useful indicator of a growing black economy in the form of off-the-books business or increasing output by informal black economy producers. It will not be possible, however, to distinguish between a growing black economy and growing errors in the allowances made by the BSO for the output of smaller producers not covered by the ACOP survey. Either of these sources could lead to an underestimate of supply; equally, if the BSO over-estimates the output of smaller producers in the formal economy a rise in black economy output could be concealed.

Nevertheless, if it were found that the greatest excesses of demand over supply occurred in those industries where experience would suggest a large proportion of black economy activity, then it might be reasonable to interpret the discrepancy as indicating in some measure the scale of such activity.

An interpretation along these lines is, however, difficult to sustain. Table 11.6 shows, for each of the thirty-nine marketed commodities, the extent to which reported supply falls short of total demand. There are ten commodities where demand is 'substantially higher' than supply (i.e. that have a positive discrepancy on average over 1978–83, higher than the average absolute value of the discrepancy for all thirty-nine accounts). These ten commodities are (in descending order):

	Percentage excess of demand over supply
Clothing and footwear	15.2
Non-ferrous metals	14.7
Motor vehicles (including parts	12.6
Ships and other vessels	10.4
Coal, coke, and other solid fuels	9.2
Timber and furniture	8.9
Instrument engineering products	8.3
Hotels and catering	7.0
Construction	6.7
Paper and board	6.4

While it is true that two of the areas thought to have the greatest amount of black economy activity (hotels and catering, and construction) appear in this list, and that a third 'prime candidate' (distribution and repair) also shows a positive though small (1.5 per cent) discrepancy, it is nonetheless clear that the list does not accord closely with the usual beliefs about the relative extent of black economy activity in different commodity and service areas. In three of the industries the bulk of the output is accounted for by large firms, which are generally felt to be less able to conduct off-the-books business (motor vehicles, ships, and paper and board). Moreover in those areas where off-the-books activity is widely reported, the discrepancy in the commodity flow accounts is generally quite small, and certainly below the 30 to 50 per cent levels that have, at times, been suggested. It would be difficult, for example, to make a case on the basis of this evidence for a percentage of off-the-books activity exceeding 12 to 15 per cent in the cases of construction, and hotels and catering, and 8 to 10 per cent in the case of distribution and repair. But since the discrepancies shown for these industries are broadly consistent with the pattern of statistical error for the commodity flow accounts as a whole, it would be equally possible to interpret the accounts as indicating that even in these sectors the extent of black economy activity is negligible.

Conclusions

The use of the difference between the income and expenditure estimates of GDP as an indicator of the size of the black economy—as suggested by MacAfee (1980)—depends on the assumption that the expenditure measure is accurate, even if the income measure is affected by the black economy. However, since retail sales data are frequently used to measure expenditure in the UK national accounts, off-the-books business might be omitted from the expenditure measure as well as from the income measure. In practice, however, using retail sales data rather than expenditure survey data does not appear to have led to understatement; if anything, the reverse might be the case. There is little evidence of large understatement even in the case of goods and services where the black economy is believed to be most significant. Furthermore, while evidence from commodity flow accounts also shows some discrepancies between the figures for expenditures and output in particular sectors, these discrepancies too are generally not large.

Chapter 12

Evidence from survey discrepancies

with Christopher A. Pissarides and Guglielmo Weber

The previous chapter has looked at the ways in which discrepancies between the figures for income and expenditure at the level of the overall economy might provide clues to the level of concealed income—and hence to the size of the black economy. It is possible to apply a similar approach to analysing the incomes and expenditures of individual households as reported to surveys such as the Family Expenditure Survey. In much the same way as the taxman might become suspicious if a taxpayer who declared a low income were found to own two houses, a yacht, and a Rolls-Royce, and to take regular holidays in the South of France, we can look to see whether surveys of household income and expenditure reveal any households that appear to be living beyond their (declared) means.

Of course, in doing so, we are limited to studying the households that have taken part in the Family Expenditure Survey, and have to base our estimates on what they have chosen to tell the survey. In both respects it is reasonable to suspect that we may not be getting the complete picture of the extent of undeclared income. People who are heavily involved in the black economy may simply fail to respond to the Family Expenditure Survey, perhaps because they do not believe the confidentiality assurances that are given, and fear that the information they give to the survey may somehow find its way back to the Inland Revenue or the Department of Health and Social Security (DHSS).[1] Other people, whilst responding to the survey, might nonetheless be aware of the implications of appearing to live beyond their means, and might adjust the amount of expenditure they report accordingly.

Both of these responses do undoubtedly give rise to a real possibility that discrepancies reported in the Family Expenditure

[1] In fact, although in this chapter we refer to analysing individual households in the Family Expenditure Survey, the survey data are completely anonymised, and there is no way in which we, or the Department sponsoring the survey, or the Inland Revenue could determine which specific households these are.

Survey do not give a full measure of the extent of tax evasion and black economy income. Both, to a greater or lesser extent, affect the two measurement approaches reported in this chapter, and should be borne in mind in interpreting their results. But the problems of non-response and expenditure under-reporting can easily be overstated. We believe that it is indeed possible to obtain some useful information about some aspects of the black economy from the analysis of survey discrepancies.

A surprisingly high proportion of the households asked to take part in the Family Expenditure Survey do indeed do so, despite the fact that it is quite a demanding exercise, involving lengthy interviews and the keeping of diary records of all expenditures by household members for a fortnight. The response rate is about 70 per cent, which compares very favourably with the level of response in other voluntary surveys. It may of course be that, despite this, the 30 per cent who do not participate in the survey engage more extensively in the black economy than those who agree to take part. But we imagine that reluctance to participate would be greater on the part of those engaged in major tax fraud than those with small amounts of moonlighting income who may not realise there is anything illegal and probably think there is nothing immoral in their failure actively to seek out a tax inspector to whom to report these earnings. It is this kind of activity, limited in scale and typically subsidiary to principal employments, that is the basis of much recent concern about the growth of black economy activity and that we believe an analysis of survey discrepancies is quite likely to identify.

This chapter looks at two possible approaches to analysing the evidence from the Family Expenditure Survey about discrepancies between reported incomes and expenditures. The first approach, reported by Dilnot and Morris (1981), calculated the gap between total reported income and total reported expenditure for individual households. Where households recorded a level of spending that was higher than their income, and where this could not be explained by purchases of expensive durable goods during the survey period or by known aspects of the household's circumstances (e.g. where the head of the household was temporarily out of work), they were categorised as 'black economy' households. Dilnot and Morris concluded that somewhere between 10 and 15 per cent of households surveyed by the 1977 Family

Expenditure Survey could, on this evidence, have been active in the black economy and under-reporting income by, on average, about £30 per week. Total concealed income across the economy as a whole would, on these figures, be equivalent to 2½ to 3 per cent of gross national product.

The second approach, which has been based on the 1982 Family Expenditure Survey, analyses households' spending on particular groups of commodities, rather than households' total spending. The aim is to see whether particular groups of the population believed likely to have particular scope for concealing earnings spend more on various products than other people with similar incomes. It appears, for example, that the self-employed spend more on household services and on food than employees who report a similar level of income. In other words, compared with employees, the self-employed appear to be enjoying a higher standard of living than their declared income warrants. In the absence of any obvious reason that the self-employed might wish to buy more household services or spend more on food than employees with similar incomes, we might conclude that the self-employed in fact have higher incomes than they report to the survey. The extent to which the self-employed under-report incomes appears on this evidence to be broadly in line with the adjustments made in the national accounts: somewhere between 10 and 20 per cent of self-employed income may, on average, be concealed.

The Dilnot and Morris approach

Dilnot and Morris (1981) analysed the relationship between total expenditures and after-tax incomes of the 7,200 households surveyed for the 1977 Family Expenditure Survey (FES). This survey collects information on expenditures, incomes, and household characteristics in some detail, and, with some adjustments to the data, permits a consistent comparison of incomes and expenditures at the household level. Two main adjustments had to be made to the data.

The first reflected the relatively short period over which expenditure records are kept: most of the FES expenditure data are based on diary entries covering a two-week period. For those products such as food that are generally purchased on a fairly continuous basis, a two-week time-span may be sufficient to gauge the household's average expenditure over a year. But household spending on other items may be less regular, and if the household records a major durable purchase during the survey fortnight (say, buying a new car, or furniture, or electrical goods), the level of household expenditure during the survey period may be considerably higher than the household's average fortnightly spending over the year as a whole. To prevent households being included in the black economy sample merely because they had happened to spend a large amount of money on durable goods during the survey fortnight, a rough adjustment was made to the data to smooth the expenditure patterns of households with very 'lumpy' expenditure patterns, setting lumpy expenditures on clothing, durables, transport, and services to the average expenditure of households of the same type.

The second adjustment was made to self-employment incomes, for which the data recorded in the Family Expenditure Survey generally refers to some time prior to the survey year (in contrast to employees' income, which is usually verified from current pay-slips). Dilnot and Morris scaled up self-employment income for individual households in the sample, on the basis of overall movements in self-employment income over the relevant periods.

Households were categorised as 'black economy' households where expenditure exceeded income by at least 20 per cent and by at least £3. This criterion was essentially pragmatic: a higher cut-off excluded households that seemed on the basis of all other information to be potential black economy candidates, while 10 to 15 per cent cut-offs brought in groups that were believed not to be. Although the number of households included in the black economy sample is obviously sensitive to the chosen cut-off level, Dilnot and Morris note that the amount of activity included is much less sensitive, because the marginal discrepancies are less than the average.

An excess of expenditures over income may, of course, occur for reasons quite unconnected with unreported income and the black economy. Some households, for example, may be running down capital in order to sustain a level of expenditure; overseas students may be living off lump-sum scholarship income; benefit recipients may be running up debts or running down savings while temporarily away from work. Where such explanations might have accounted for the excess of income over expenditure, Dilnot and Morris did not include these households in their 'lower bound' sample of black economy households. But they also report an 'upper bound' estimate, including pensioner and unemployed households and others that had been excluded from the lower bound because their reported excess of expenditure over income might well have arisen for reasons that had nothing to do with the black economy.

In total, about 10 per cent of households reported an excess of expenditure over income that could not be explained by their particular circumstances. These households were included in the lower bound estimates shown in Table 12.1. About 15 per cent of households came into the upper bound estimate. On average each of these households was spending about £30 more per week than it was earning. Such a level of black economy income would add about $2\frac{1}{2}$ to 3 per cent to gross national product if repeated in the population at large.

TABLE 12.1

'Black Economy Households'
in the 1977 Family Expenditure Survey

	'Lower bound' sample	'Upper bound' sample
Number of households as proportion of FES sample	9.6%	14.8%
Average discrepancy between income and expenditure	£31 p.w.	£30 p.w.
Approximate size of the black economy	£3.2 billion	£4.2 billion
● as percentage of 1977 GNP	2.3%	3.0%

Source: Dilnot and Morris, 1981, p. 66.

What kinds of households figured most prominently in the sample of black economy households identified by Dilnot and Morris? Table 12.2 shows that about three-quarters of the lower bound sample were households where the head was a full-time employee, and about a quarter were households where the head was self-employed. In nearly two-thirds of the black economy

TABLE 12.2

Occupation and Economic Status for 'Lower Bound'
Black Economy Sample

OCCUPATION	HEAD OF HOUSEHOLD			
	Self-employed (%)	Full-time employee (%)	Part-time employee (%)	All (%)
Professional and technical	2	7	–	9
Administrative and managerial	7	9	–	16
Skilled manual	9	28	1	39
Semi-skilled manual	2	15	3	20
Unskilled manual	–	3	–	4
Others[a]	1	10	2	12
All	22	71	6	100

[a] Teachers, clerical workers, shop assistants, members of HM Forces, retired, unoccupied.

Source: Dilnot and Morris, 1981, p. 67.

households, the head of the household was working in a skilled or semi-skilled manual occupation.

The proportion of self-employed households in the Dilnot and Morris black economy sample was much greater than in the population at large. Only about 7 per cent of households surveyed by the 1977 Family Expenditure Survey had a self-employed head of household, but such households comprised 22 per cent of the lower bound black economy sample. As an indication of how likely particular types of people were to participate in black economy activity, Dilnot and Morris calculated the 'participation ratios' shown in Table 12.3. These are the ratios between the observed number of households of each type in the 'black economy' sample and the expected number if participation were equally likely for all groups of the population. A ratio in excess of 1.0 indicates a set of characteristics that are positively associated with activity in the black economy. Overall, Table 12.3 shows that the self-employed

TABLE 12.3

Participation Ratios by Occupation and Employee Status

OCCUPATION	HEAD OF HOUSEHOLD			
	Self-employed	Full-time employee	Part-time employee	All
Professional and technical	1.2	0.8	0.9	0.8
Administrative and managerial	2.3	0.9	1.6	1.2
Teachers	0	0.7	0.5	0.5
Other non-manual	3.3	1.0	1.0	1.0
Skilled manual	2.5	1.0	1.5	1.1
Semi-skilled manual	2.9	1.0	1.4	1.0
Unskilled manual	1.5	0.9	0.5	0.7
All	2.2	0.9	1.0	1.0

Source: Dilnot and Morris, 1981, p. 69.

were much more likely than other groups to appear in the black economy sample. Full-time employees, especially employees in professional, technical, administrative, managerial, or teaching occupations, were considerably less likely than average to be active in the black economy. People in skilled or semi-skilled manual occupations seemed to have greater scope for black economy activity than people in unskilled occupations.

The pattern of black economy activity identified by Dilnot and Morris seems to correspond quite well to the problem areas for tax evasion and black economy earnings outlined in earlier chapters. The self-employed have greater opportunity to evade tax than do employees, and people with skills appear to be more likely than those without skills to find opportunities for black economy work. The estimates of the scale of the black economy—as opposed to the pattern of black economy activity—that derive from this method are of course vulnerable to the arguments about non-response and expenditure concealment noted at the start of this chapter. But even if these problems are judged not to be serious, a more fundamental problem is the essentially arbitrary nature of the cut-off criterion employed. Does a 20 per cent excess of expenditure over income in the survey fortnight necessarily imply anything about undeclared income—or might it not be counterbalanced by a 20 per cent excess of income over expenditure in another period? Similarly, is there any reason why all people active in the black economy should spend more than they earn? Some could save all or part of their undeclared earnings, which would then mean that they might not appear in the black economy sample. These problems have prompted consideration of a second approach to the analysis of household survey data, looked at in the next section.

The expenditure equations approach

In contrast to the Dilnot and Morris approach, this 'expenditure equations' approach starts out from the initial assumption that some groups of the population have greater scope for concealment of income and for moonlighting work than other groups. It might plausibly be argued that self-employed painters and decorators, for example, have greater scope for concealing a proportion of their income than civil servants or the employees of large companies. The expenditure equations approach compares the relationship between income and spending on particular goods for different groups of the population. The differences in income/expenditure relationships for different groups that cannot be explained by differences in family characteristics are then interpreted as implying differences in the level of concealed income for those groups. If we compare the behaviour of potential evaders with the behaviour of groups believed to have little opportunity for income concealment we can then make an estimate of the overall level of concealed income in the economy.

The main focus of the work reported here is a comparison between the reported spending behaviour of the self-employed and of employees. Our hypothesis is that the self-employed have much greater opportunity for concealing income from the tax authorities than do employees, and that this will be evident from a comparison of their spending patterns with those of employees. At the same levels of reported income, for example, the self-employed may spend more on particular goods than otherwise similar employees do. Their more 'affluent' consumption pattern may give us sufficient information to enable us to estimate what the 'true' incomes of the self-employed might be, and hence to estimate the amount of income they conceal.

The approach is based on the estimation of the relationships between reported income levels (Y) and expenditure on particular goods (C), as shown in Figure 12.1. These relationships show that households with higher incomes have, on average, a higher level of spending on various groups of commodities. This relationship will vary for different commodities: spending on food and other 'necessities' rises less rapidly with income than does spending on services, entertainment, and other 'luxuries'. It will also be affected by a range of other factors: the number of adults and children in the household, the age of the head of the household, the type of housing tenure, and the season of the year may all affect the level and pattern of household spending.

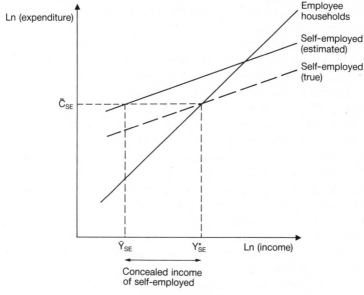

FIGURE 12.1

Consumption Functions for Employee and Self-Employed Households

In addition, quite apart from the question of unreported income, we might expect the income/expenditure relationships for the self-employed to differ in some respects from those for employees, because of the greater variability and uncertainty of self-employment income. The consumption pattern of households with highly variable incomes might be expected not to follow every temporary rise and fall in income, but to reflect instead the long-term average income that the household expects ('permanent income'). Rises in permanent income might affect consumption, but the relationship between one year's income level and the level of consumption might be less strong.

The marginal propensity to consume estimated from current income data would thus be lower for households such as the self-employed with highly variable incomes than for employees with stable incomes: in Figure 12.1, the slope of the consumption function for the self-employed would be less steep than for other groups. While the method used does permit such a difference in the marginal propensity to consume of the self-employed and other groups, it rests on the assumption that in other respects the consumption patterns and preferences of the self-employed are the same as other groups with similar family characteristics.

Consumption functions were estimated for employees and the self-employed in two separate occupational groups: 'white collar' occupations (including managerial, professional and clerical occupations, teachers, and shop assistants) and 'blue collar' occupations (skilled, semi-skilled, and unskilled manual occupations). Separate functions were estimated for three principal groups of expenditures: food, drink, and tobacco; 'pre-commitments' (rent, mortgage interest, rates, and water charges); and 'other non-durables' (including fuels, power, some non-durable goods, travel, and services). In addition, for the white collar group, further equations were estimated for spending on food alone and on services. (Since alcoholic drink and fuel are two items that it is sometimes suggested the self-employed are able to obtain as business expenditure, we wanted to see what effect leaving them out of the analysis would have.)

The relationships between consumption and income were estimated in log:log (constant elasticity) form, with additional variables including the age of the head of the household (and a squared term, to allow a 'life-cycle' profile of spending), household composition variables, dummies to reflect the type of housing tenure and region, and seasonal dummies. For each group of occupations and expenditures, two different equations were estimated. In the first, both the intercept term and the marginal

TABLE 12.4

Consumption Equations, 1982, for 'White Collar' Households

Equation number	Dependent variable: ln(expenditure) on:	Constant	Self-employed (SE)	Ln(net income) (Y)	Y×SE	R̄²
1	Food, drink, and tobacco	0.25 (1.7)	1.11 (5.5)*	0.31 (12.9)*	-0.22 (5.0)*	0.40
2	Food, drink, and tobacco	0.44 (3.1)*	0.11 (3.5)*	0.26 (11.8)*		0.40
3	Food	0.11 (0.8)	1.11 (6.0)*	0.28 (12.8)*	-0.22 (5.6)*	0.47
4	Food	0.20 (1.6)	0.096 (3.3)*	0.23 (11.4)*		0.46
5	Pre-commitments (rent, rates, etc.)	0.96 (5.8)*	0.89 (3.8)*	0.36 (12.8)*	-0.19 (3.8)*	0.59
6	Pre-commitments	1.12 (7.0)*	0.018 (0.5)	0.31 (12.4)*		0.59
7	Other non-durables (including services, etc.)	0.03 (0.2)	0.33 (1.3)	0.48 (15.7)*	-0.081 (1.5)	0.35
8	Other non-durables (including services, etc.)	0.1 (0.6)	-0.03 (0.9)	0.46 (16.8)*		0.35
9	Services	-2.85 (10.0)*	0.78 (1.9)	0.65 (13.4)*	-0.16 (1.8)	0.23
10	Services	-2.71 (9.8)*	0.052 (0.8)	0.61 (14.0)*		0.23

propensity to consume out of reported income were es
separately for self-employed and employed households, so t
estimated consumption functions could appear as in Figure 1
the second equation of each pair, self-employed and em,
households were constrained to have the same marginal prop
to consume, although the intercept term was allowed to vary
estimated equations are shown in Table 12.4 for white
occupations and Table 12.5 for blue collar occupations.

Looking at the second equation in each pair, it is clear that
are some statistically significant differences between the leve
consumption of self-employed households and empl
households, at each level of income. The dummy vari
identifying self-employed households is significant at the 5 per
level in four out of the eight equations estimated in this form.
each of the four equations where the self-employment variabl
significant it has a positive sign, indicating that self-employ
households spend, on average, more on those goods than employ
households with similar income levels. On the basis that we cann
see any reason that, on average, self-employed households shou.
spend more than employee households with the same level of tru
income, we may interpret the results of these equations as evidenc
that the self-employed have higher levels of income than the
report to the Family Expenditure Survey. (Indeed, if anything we
might have expected the average consumption of the self-employed
to be lower than that of employees. Many employees, for example,
belong to occupational pension schemes, and their pension
contributions are not included in our income data. On the other
hand, the incomes of the self-employed include any money they
may later pay to private pension schemes.)

The extent of this income under-reporting can be calculated from
the first equation in each pair. These equations have the form:

$$C = Za + b_1X + (b_2 + b_3X) Y \tag{1}$$

where C = ln(expenditure)
Z = household characteristics
X = 1 if head of household self-employed,
0 otherwise
Y = ln(income).

Notes: In addition, each equation included variables representing the age (and age^2) of the head of household, the number of adults, children and tax units in the household, dummy variables for council and private tenants, mortgage payments, and region, and seasonal dummies. As in Table 12.5 the coefficients on these variables are not reported here for reasons of space, but further details are available on request from the authors. t-statistics are shown in parentheses below the coefficients; an asterisk shows coefficients significant at the 5 per cent level.

TABLE 12.5

Consumption Equations, 1982, for 'Blue Collar' Households

Equation number	Dependent variable: ln(expenditure) on:	Constant	Self-employed (SE)	Ln(net income) (Y)	Y×SE	$\bar{R}^2$
11	Food, drink, and tobacco	0.66 (6.7)*	-0.002 (0.01)	0.30 (17.1)*	0.021 (0.4)	0.50
12	Food, drink, and tobacco	0.66 (6.7)*	0.089 (3.5)*	0.30 (17.7)*		0.50
13	Pre-commitments	0.81 (6.7)*	0.41 (1.6)	0.25 (11.8)*	-0.076 (1.2)	0.58
14	Pre-commitments	0.83 (6.9)*	0.085 (2.7)*	0.25 (11.9)*		0.58
15	Other non-durables	0.22 (1.6)	-0.24 (0.8)	0.53 (22.0)*	0.065 (1.0)	0.40
16	Other non-durables	0.21 (1.5)	0.040 (1.1)	0.53 (22.8)*		0.40

Note: See notes to Table 12.4.

In effect, each of these equations represents two consumption functions—one for the self-employed households and the other for employees—as in Figure 12.1. We assume the employee consumption function to have been estimated using the true levels of income; the consumption function for the self-employed, however, has been estimated using income data that we assume have been systematically understated. The estimated consumption function for the self-employed, then, lies somewhat to the left of the 'true' consumption function for the self-employed. If we further assume that the consumption of self-employed households at true average income is the same as the consumption of similar employee households (although the marginal propensity to consume may differ because of greater income variability for the self-employed) then the intersection of the true self-employed and employee consumption functions would occur at mean self-employed income. In practice, the estimated consumption function for the self-employed in all the equations except one lies to the left of the true consumption function. Hence true self-employed income is, on average, estimated to be above reported income.

The extent of income under-reporting by the self-employed was derived from the estimated equations in the following way. Our assumption that the average consumption of self-employed households at the true average level of self-employment income is the same as the average consumption of other households with similar characteristics at the same income implies that:

$$\overline{C}_{SE} = \overline{Z}_{SE}a + b_2 Y_{SE}^* \tag{2}$$

where $\overline{C}_{SE}$ = average expenditure of self-employed households
$\overline{Z}_{SE}$ = average household characteristics of self-employed households
$\overline{Y}_{SE}^*$ = true self-employed income.

The estimates of equation (1), on the other hand, imply that:

$$\overline{C}_{SE} = \overline{Z}_{SE}a + b_1 + (b_2 + b_3)\overline{Y}_{SE} \tag{3}$$

where $\overline{Y}_{SE}$ = average reported income of self-employed households.

Equating (2) and (3) we get:

$$b_2 Y^*_{SE} = b_1 + (b_2 + b_3) \bar{Y}_{SE} \tag{4}$$

Re-arranging equation (4) allows us to calculate the percentage under-reporting of self-employment incomes as:

$$Y^*_{SE} - \bar{Y}_{SE} = (b_1 + b_3 \bar{Y}_{SE}) / b_2$$

Estimates of the mean understatement of income by the self-employed derived in this way from Tables 12.4 and 12.5 and the corresponding mean overstatement of consumption (in relation to reported income levels) are given in Table 12.6. These show a considerable range. The four estimates that correspond to the four equations where the self-employment dummy was statistically significant all suggest understatement of income by the self-employed in the range 30 to 36 per cent. But the other four suggest much lower levels of understatement, of 8 per cent or less. (One estimate, for white collar households' spending on other non-

TABLE 12.6

Estimates of Concealed Income, 1982, Self-Employed Households

	'Excess consumption' of self-employed households at average income[a] (%)	Income concealed by self-employed households (%)
'White collar' households		
Food, drink, and tobacco	11.1*	36
Food	9.6*	34
Pre-commitments	1.8	5
Other non-durables	-3	-6
Services	5.2	8
'Blue collar' households		
Food, drink, and tobacco	8.9*	30
Pre-commitments	8.5*	34
Other non-durables	4.0	8

[a] An asterisk indicates that 'excess consumption' is statistically significant at the 5% level.

durables, suggests overstatement, but the difference between self-employed and employee households is not statistically significant.) The average understatement is about 18 per cent.

The equations for households' spending on food are perhaps most likely to produce reliable estimates of the extent of under-reporting. Pre-commitments cannot be varied easily, and may have only a very indirect relationship to income in any particular year. Spending on rates and water rates, for example, cannot be adjusted quickly in response to changes in income. The services equation, while containing many spending items that, like food, can be adjusted quickly to changes in income and other household circumstances, also contains some items of spending that have a durable-type component. Servicing a car, for example, is in some respects rather like buying a durable good with an expected life of one or two years. The food equations suggest an average understatement of self-employment incomes of around 30 per cent.

One last adjustment needs to be made to these figures before a final measure of the extent of concealed income earned by the self-employed can result. This reflects the difference in the periods to which the income data in the Family Expenditure Survey refer. Most of the self-employment income data in the Family Expenditure Survey relate to a period some fifteen months or so prior to the survey date, although some are based on current income estimates. On average, the self-employment incomes in the 1982 FES could be understated by perhaps 10 per cent or so in relation to employment incomes, simply because of the different dates to which the income data refer.

Taking this adjustment into account, the estimates of concealed self-employment income based on the four equations where the self-employment dummy was significant would average about 20 per cent. Across all eight estimates the extent of income concealed by the self-employed appears to be smaller—about 10 per cent. A level of concealed income within this range would be broadly consistent with the adjustments for evasion that are made in calculating total self-employment income in the national accounts. In 1980–2, for example, this adjustment amounted to about one-seventh (i.e. about 14 per cent) of the published item.

Conclusions

The research reported in this chapter shows that incomes and expenditures reported to the Family Expenditure Survey do indeed show signs of discrepancies that may be due to some income being concealed. The Dilnot and Morris results suggest that about 10 or 15 per cent of households might have some form of concealed income, but that the total amount of hidden income was not large—perhaps $2\frac{1}{2}$ or 3 per cent of GNP. The second approach has looked in more detail at the unreported incomes of the self-employed, the group identified by Dilnot and Morris as being most likely to have hidden income. The results suggest that self-employed incomes could be understated by between 10 and 20 per cent, a level that is broadly consistent with the level of understatement assumed in the UK national accounts.

Part IV
The wider shadow economy

Chapter 13

The wider shadow economy

Most of the attempts at measuring the importance of parts of the shadow economy have concentrated on the market transactions that constitute the black economy—transactions involving tax evasion or that are illegal for other reasons. The monetary approach to measuring the black economy, for example, is aimed at estimating the value of unrecorded cash transactions, while the approach based on national accounts discrepancies is designed to identify unrecorded factor incomes. But the market transactions within the black economy are only part of the much wider range of productive activities that occur outside the formal economy, and that therefore constitute the shadow economy. Many services, particularly to children and the elderly, are provided through voluntary organisations, and many other civic activities are based upon voluntary labour. Neither the labour inputs nor the output of these organisations and activities are the subject of market transactions, and their value is not included in gross domestic product (GDP) or other national accounts statistics. Similarly, many productive activities take place within the 'household economy'. Such activities, ranging from productive 'domestic' activities such as cooking, cleaning, childcare, and so on, to a wide range of do-it-yourself production activities including car maintenance, painting and decorating, and home-brewing, are not reflected in the UK national accounts statistics.

Nevertheless productive activities within the non-market shadow economy clearly comprise a sizeable proportion of the total production of goods and services. Estimates have been made of the aggregate value of household production in the US. As the survey by Hawrylyshyn (1976) shows, these vary widely, depending on the method used to assess the value of non-market production activities, but all suggest that the value of household production is substantial, equivalent to somewhere between 20 and 45 per cent of measured GDP.

With a non-market sector of this size, it is clear that any process of substitution between the formal and informal non-market economies could have a not insignificant effect on the level and pattern of economic activity within the formal economy. Economic problems such as unemployment could be exacerbated by a comparatively small shift towards production within households rather than within the formal economy. Many of the factors that encourage growth of the black economy may also affect the division of activities between the formal economy and the non-market shadow economy, and many of the public policy issues that arise in the context of the black economy have their counterpart in the wider shadow economy too.

Just as high tax rates in the formal economy may be an incentive to 'black' economic activity, so they may also encourage production within the household. When the cost of motor servicing is increased by both value added tax (VAT) on the garage's bill and taxes on the labour time involved, some car owners may cut down on the frequency with which their car is serviced, and some may seek to have the job done 'tax-free' in the black economy. Others may choose to do the job themselves, supplying their own labour free (and untaxed) and avoiding the VAT on garage bills. When the servicing was performed in the formal economy its value was included in GDP, and even when it was performed in the black economy it is widely agreed that it *should* have been included in GDP. However, when it is performed on a self-service basis within the household economy it is not counted as part of GDP.

What is more, in the UK at least, little attempt seems to have been made to assess the significance of possible substitutions between household and formal economy production. It is perhaps true that there are large areas of the household economy where the possibility of substitution with the formal economy is limited. But there are other activities, such as home improvements and decoration, where the potential for substitution between the formal economy and do-it-yourself (DIY) in the household economy seems much greater.

As with the black economy, so in the household economy, the issues raised by such substitutions are not simply ones of measurement. Gershuny (1983), for example, has drawn attention to the considerable expansion in the opportunities for self-service provision of goods and services over the past few decades. In a relatively short space of time the technology of household production has been transformed by a range of consumer durable goods (e.g. washing machines, vacuum cleaners, power tools), and by a range of new materials that have substantially 'de-skilled' many home maintenance and other DIY tasks. The development of new techniques for self-service provision within households may simply reflect a process of autonomous technological development. It is possible that the widening scope for substitution away from the formal economy would have occurred even if no incentive had been provided by the tax system. But it is alternatively possible, and potentially a matter of public policy concern, that some of the substitutions that have taken place have been responses to the rates of taxation in force. Clearly, from the point of view of efficient utilisation of national resources it could be undesirable if (possibly costly) changes in the technology of household production were taking place purely as a response to the incentives generated by taxation within the formal economy. In this sense, the issue of substitution between the household and formal economies has clear parallels with public policy concerns about the possible efficiency costs of production in the black economy.

Chapter 14

The household economy

A considerable amount of productive economic activity takes place within households, producing goods and services for the benefit of household members. Household economic activity does not involve market transactions and is not reflected in gross domestic product (GDP) statistics.

This chapter considers whether it is possible to value this household production, so that it can be compared with the production of goods and services in the formal economy. The first section defines what is meant by household production, and outlines criteria for distinguishing productive activities from other household activities. The second section considers the economic factors that might enter into decision-making about household production. It is suggested that important factors include the time required for household production and the 'opportunity cost' of the time used. The final section considers whether those factors identified as being relevant to the production decision provide any basis for valuing household production.

Definition of 'household production'

It might seem a straightforward matter to define the household activities that should be included in a measure of household production. Most people would unhesitatingly agree that cleaning, cooking, and putting up shelves should be counted in household production, while watching television and playing 'Scrabble' should not. But the border-line cases are less easy to define (for example, gardening may be viewed either as a relaxing hobby or as a means of obtaining cheap vegetables), and when probed a little the notion of 'productive activity' turns out to be surprisingly elastic. Both eating and sleeping may be held to be activities necessary for the reproduction of labour power—'recharging the batteries' as it were—and hence an indispensable element in production in both the formal and shadow economies. With only a

160

little violence to the concept of production it may seem possible therefore to count time spent eating and sleeping as part of the total time devoted to household production.

Stretching the point a little more, however, allows almost anything to be counted as a productive activity. If sleeping is a necessary element in the preparation of the human mind and body for the next day's work, then by the same token leisure activities may be just as important and 'productive'. All work and no play may not only make Jack a dull boy; it may also in time make him a less efficient and less productive member of the workforce. With a little imagination therefore—and a touch of cynicism, too, perhaps—a case could be made for describing all human activity as, in one sense or another, productive. But in the process, the notion of production has taken on a meaning rather different from the one that we started with, and has lost the ability to distinguish between activities that common sense tells us are productive, such as painting and decorating, and those, such as spending an evening in the pub, that common sense tells us produce very little.

How, then, to draw the boundary between household production and other activities within the household? One possible criterion might be whether the activity was undertaken for pleasure, or whether it was undertaken solely for the benefits that would result from it. Watching 'Grandstand' on television on Saturday afternoon is done for pleasure and is therefore 'unproductive'; mowing the lawn instead is not pleasurable, but is productive. Such a 'medicinal' view of production is, however, clearly unsatisfactory. It is wildly at odds with the way we treat the formal economy, where the fact that some people enjoy their jobs has no effect on the estimates of gross domestic product. Equally, within the household economy, some people may enjoy cooking and others may not, but the output—a meal—may be the same in each case.

A more satisfactory definition is provided by the 'third-person' criterion suggested by Hawrylyshyn (1977) and Hill (1979). Productive activities are defined by Hawrylyshyn as activities 'which may be done by someone other than the person benefitting therefrom'. The question should be asked: can one hire labour to achieve the same results? If so, then the activity is productive; if not, it should not be counted in the sum total of goods and services produced in the household. 'In effect, this criterion is exactly the same as that always used by national income accounts (namely the market criterion) simply extended to its full logical possibilities.' (Hawrylyshyn, 1977.)

As Hill (1979) observes, the production of goods is easily recognised as a productive activity, as is the production of 'services performed on goods' (e.g. when a good is transported, repaired, cleaned, or re-decorated). It is straightforward to see that someone could be employed to grow vegetables in one's garden, or to clean or re-decorate the house. The point where the third-person criterion has to work harder is in the identification of 'services affecting persons'—medical treatment, education, entertainment, and so on. Such services are 'changes in the physical or mental conditions of human beings which can be realised by others'. Non-service activities not included in the total of household production are those such as 'eating, drinking, sleeping, reading, studying, taking exercise or recreation which an individual cannot pay someone to do on his behalf no matter how valuable his own time is'. Thus, for example, I could pay someone to cook for me, and therefore the output from my own cooking counts as production, but I cannot employ anyone to eat my meals on my behalf, and so the time I spend eating does not count as time spent on production.

Production decisions in the household economy

Where the boundary between the formal economy and the household economy lies depends fundamentally on how the production decision within households is made. On what basis do people choose to do some things themselves (household production), and to have others done by someone else (formal economy)?

Hawrylyshyn (1977), drawing on earlier work by Becker (1965) and Lancaster (1966), has argued that the allocation of time is the crucial element in this decision. The time that an individual spends on household production is time that could alternatively have been spent on leisure activities, on personal care, sleep, and other 'necessary' human functions, or on work in the formal economy. Since, for all individuals, time is in fixed supply—a day is always twenty-four hours long, and no longer—the time allocation problem is one of allocating the time available between these competing activities.

The various alternative uses of time are shown in Figure 14.1. A certain irreducible minimum of time will need to be devoted to sleep, personal care, eating, and other necessary functions. The time remaining may be allocated to one of three uses—market work, domestic work, or leisure. All are assumed to yield utility to the individual. Market work and domestic work both contribute to the production of 'basic commodities' (childcare, eating, shelter, and so on) which themselves yield utility; more leisure time is desirable in its own right. The problem of allocating time is thus one of maximising the utility from these three uses of time, subject to the fixed constraint on the amount of time available.

Time, in this model, will only be allocated to household work if the utility resulting from additional household work is greater than

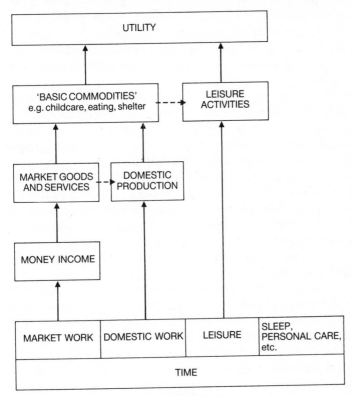

FIGURE 14.1

The Allocation of Time to Different Activities

the utility resulting from additional time devoted to leisure or to work in the formal economy. In general, a rational utility-maximising individual will allocate time between the three activities in such a way that the marginal utility derived from spending an extra hour on each would be the same. The value to the rational individual of the marginal hour devoted to housework is the same as the value of the marginal hour devoted to leisure and of the marginal hour devoted to paid work in the formal economy. If it were not, a re-allocation of time could increase the individual's utility.

This result—which has obvious parallels with the economic theory of the profit-maximising firm—can be used in two ways. Firstly, it can be used to make predictions about the household production decisions of various groups of people—for example, about how the different opportunities for formal economy work open to different people may affect the amount of household production they choose to do. Secondly, as the next section shows, it may provide a basis for estimating the value of household production.

As an example of the first kind of application, consider the choice between spending time on household work and spending time on work in the formal economy, to earn money to pay for the household work to be done by someone else. One such choice might be a mother's decision about whether to employ a nanny or childminder, paying for the costs of childcare out of her earnings from a job in the formal economy. It can be seen that paying for childcare to be undertaken by someone else, rather than within the household economy, will seem a more attractive option if she can earn more by spending time working in the formal economy than she would save by performing the childcare herself rather than employing a childminder.

It would seem probable that people whose potential income from work in the formal economy was high in relation to the cost of a childminder would be more likely to employ a childminder than people whose potential income in the formal economy was low. Secondly, if the costs of employing a childminder are increased by National Insurance contributions and other non-wage costs of employing labour, or if the potential income from work in the formal economy is reduced by income tax, the scope for earning enough in the formal economy to pay for a childminder will be reduced. Tax and National Insurance contributions will thus tend to encourage production outside the formal economy.

However, it is clear that economic considerations will be only one of the factors entering into the decision about whether to employ a childminder or to look after one's own children. Mothers may wish to look after their own children, or may feel that a childminder is an inadequate replacement for their own childcare. Women and mothers also come under various social pressures ('a woman's place is in the home', etc.) that may deter them from taking a job and employing a childminder. Alternatively, a job in the formal economy may provide satisfaction over and above the wages earned, and some mothers may choose to take a job even if it barely covers the cost of a childminder.

The choice between household production and an alternative from the formal economy, illustrated by the example of employing a childminder, involves a fairly straightforward choice between performing certain activities oneself or employing someone else to perform broadly similar activities instead. Many possible substitutions between formal economy production and household production follow this pattern—employing someone to do the cooking and washing up, employing someone to do household cleaning, household repairs, painting and decorating, and so on. Other possible substitutions involve completely different processes in the household and formal economies. Restaurant meals can be substituted for cooking, laundry services for washing clothes, and so on. These substitutions too can be analysed within the time allocation framework. The choice between household and formal economy provision would, as before, depend on a comparison between the wages that could be earned in the formal economy—the 'opportunity cost' of labour time in the household economy—and the market price of the service if purchased from the formal economy.

One group of substitutions, however, that are less easy to analyse using the time allocation model are those that do not involve any saving of time. Employing a chauffeur, for example, may not reduce the amount of time spent travelling; being shaved by a barber may actually take longer than shaving oneself at home. The time allocation model may suggest that, other things being equal, formal economy services involving no savings in time may be less frequently used than those that involve domestic labour-saving.

STAFFORDSHIRE
POLYTECHNIC
LIBRARY

But it is clear that the reasons for such substitutions must be sought outside the framework provided by the time allocation model.

The value of household production

The amount of time that is spent on productive activities within the household economy is substantial. According to a time-budget study conducted amongst 450 households in Reading in 1973, women who were not employed in the formal economy spent about forty-two hours per week on domestic work, childcare, and shopping. Women who were employed in the formal economy worked an average twenty-five hours in the household economy, in addition to an average twenty-five hours of paid work. Men's work was much more heavily concentrated in the formal economy—about thirty hours a week paid work compared with only about nine hours of household work. (Bullock, Dickens, Shapcott, and Steadman, 1974.) Overall, it would appear from this study that the average adult spent nearly as much time on domestic work, childcare, and shopping as on work in the formal economy. (Table 14.1.)

TABLE 14.1

Time Spent on Household Work, Reading Study, 1973, hours per week, per adult

	Men	Working women	Non-working women
Domestic	6.2	20.4	32.3
Childcare	0.8	1.1	5.7
Shopping, use of services	1.8	3.2	4.3
Total household work	8.8	24.7	42.3
Formal economy work	30.0	25.2	0.4

Source: Bullock, Dickens, Shapcott, and Steadman, 1974.

The amount of time devoted to household production is a clear indication of the importance of household production in contributing to the total of goods and services produced in the economy. However, a number of economists have sought to go further, and to estimate the value of household production in monetary terms, so as to be able to compare the value of household production with the statistics of formal economy gross domestic product.

Most of the estimates of the value of household production that have so far been made have been for the US, and the answers obtained have covered a wide range. Hawrylyshyn's (1976) survey reports results ranging from about 20 per cent to about 45 per cent of measured gross national product (GNP), but concludes that the balance of the evidence suggests a figure of around one-third of GNP.

By contrast, it appears that only one attempt has been made to estimate the value of household services in the UK, by Clark (1958). Clark based his estimates on statistics of the cost of upkeep for children and adults in institutional homes, and also concluded that the aggregate value of household services in the UK in 1956 was equivalent to about one-third of measured UK gross national product.

The US estimates have not followed Clark's approach, but instead are based on valuations of the time spent on household production activities. Two competing methodologies have been employed to value the time inputs. One is the opportunity cost approach, which sets the value of work done at home equal to the income the person could earn from alternatively spending the time working in the formal economy. The other is the market cost approach, which uses the cost of employing someone to do the housework to determine its value.

The opportunity cost approach can be seen to derive from the model of decision-making outlined in the previous section. This model led to the conclusion that a rational individual will allocate the time available between household production, paid work in the formal economy, and leisure so that the marginal utility from time in each allocation is the same. The opportunity cost approach extends this result to the further conclusion that the value of the marginal hour's household production is equal to its opportunity cost—in other words, equal to what could be earned from an hour's additional employment in the formal economy. This relationship, which is strictly only true at the margin, is then used to value all time spent on household production.

Valuing non-market time at the market wage has become a

familiar procedure in cost-benefit studies, especially of transport projects, where a value has to be attached to the saving of time from a new road, for example. It is recognised even in those applications to involve problems; in particular, if individuals are not free to vary the hours they work, the opportunity cost of time may differ significantly from their hourly wage rate. However, whatever its merits in transport cost-benefit applications, it is clear that the opportunity cost approach has serious deficiencies as a method of valuing household production. These are well summarised in Hawrylyshyn (1977).

The first problem is in the use of a relationship that is true at the margin to value intra-marginal time use. The opportunity cost of an *extra* hour devoted to any activity is equal to the market wage, but the theory does not imply that all the hours spent on domestic work should be valued at the market wage rate. This problem can reasonably be ignored in transport cost-benefit analyses where the savings of time are typically small. It cannot be ignored so readily in the valuation of the substantial amount of time spent on household production.

A second and possibly even more serious objection to an opportunity cost valuation of labour inputs to household production is that some people may derive satisfaction from doing productive household tasks. Do-it-yourself (DIY) work or gardening, for example, may be undertaken solely for the value of the home improvements or vegetables that they produce, but many people regard DIY and gardening as a form of relaxation, undertaken at least in part for the enjoyment that they derive from the activity. Where household production is undertaken partly for pleasure there is no longer any need for the value of the output produced to bear any relationship to the labour time expended.

This objection rules out the opportunity cost method of valuing the labour time expended on household production for a wide range of household activities, quite plausibly including childcare, shopping, and cooking, in addition to DIY and gardening. While some may regard all these activities as chores, others may enjoy doing them, and may be prepared to do them even if the opportunity cost of their labour considerably exceeds the value of goods and services that result.

A similar objection can be advanced to the second method of valuing household labour time—the 'market cost' approach. This method uses the cost of employing someone else to do household work as a measure of the value of the goods and services produced. It is in any case hard to see what relationship might be thought to exist between the hourly cost of domestic servants and the value of output resulting from unpaid domestic labour. The possibility that people might enjoy doing some parts of household work means that they might be prepared to devote a considerable amount of time, even rather unproductively, to such work. I may, for example, enjoy wallpapering, and may be prepared to take ten times as long to do it as a professional paper-hanger would need. But there is no reason then to want to value my paper-hanging at ten times that of someone working more swiftly and efficiently. There seems to be no rationale at all for valuing actual time-budget data using the hourly cost of hired labour, as the 'market cost' approach seeks to do.

In conclusion, then, neither valuation method seems likely to yield a soundly-based estimate of the value of household production from time-budget data about domestic labour times. An adequate basis does not appear to exist for comparing the output of the household economy with GDP in the formal economy. The best, though undoubtedly imperfect, indicator of the relative importance of the two areas of economic activity is probably provided by the simple comparison of labour hours, with which this section began.

In any case, the purpose of achieving more polished estimates of the relative magnitudes of the formal and household economies is far from clear. What is important from the point of view of economic analysis and policy is the relationship at the margin between the two economies, and the extent of substitution from one to the other. It is this aspect of the household economy that is considered further in the next chapter.

Chapter 15

Substitution and the household economy

The previous chapter has indicated the extent of productive activities within the household economy. Households undertake a wide range of activities that also could, in principle, be provided through the market; the labour time devoted to the production of goods and services within the household economy could be almost as much as the labour time devoted to production in the formal economy. In addition, activities in the 'communal economy' (voluntary organisations, helping neighbours, etc.) extend still further the goods and services that are produced outside the formal economy.

From the point of view of economic policy, the relative magnitudes of production in the formal, household, and communal economies are of little importance. What are far more important are the interactions between them; in particular, whether the formal, household, and communal economies form distinct and separate spheres of activity, or whether there is scope for substitution between them. In other words, are there one group of activities that are exclusively performed within households, and a different group that are usually obtained through the formal economy? Or is the balance of activity between the household and formal economies something that varies from household to household, and that can be affected by economic conditions (unemployment, the state of the business cycle, etc.) or incentives (tax rates on goods and services, after-tax income, etc.)?

This chapter considers three aspects of possible substitution between the formal and household economies. The first is the effect of income on the amount of 'housework' done within the household economy. Do households with a higher opportunity cost of time (higher-income households) spend less time on housework? The second aspect is the growth of 'do-it-yourself' (DIY) home decorating and improvements. Has the growth of DIY reflected substitution away from the formal economy (builders and decorators, etc.), perhaps because of higher labour costs or taxes in the formal economy? Or is it instead a reflection of growing affluence—part of a boom in home improvements generally? The third issue considered is the participation of the unemployed in the household economy. What scope do the unemployed have to compensate for their loss of earnings in the formal economy by increased unpaid productive activity in the household economy?

Household work and income

The theory of time allocation outlined in the previous chapter would predict that households with high hourly earnings in the formal economy would tend to spend less time on household production and proportionately more on the alternative services that can be purchased from the formal economy. The extent to which the level of income affects the balance of resources devoted to economic activity in the formal and household economies may be taken as an indicator both of the possible scope for substitution between the formal and household economies, and of the extent to which the substitution could be responsive to economic factors.

In the case of domestic housework it is clear that, while a straightforward inverse relationship between the amount of time spent on domestic work and the level of household income may have existed in the past, the present position is considerably less clear-cut. Gershuny (1983) presents some time-budget data for the amount of time spent on domestic work by middle-class and working-class housewives over the period 1937 to 1975. In 1937 the working-class housewives spent roughly twice as much time as middle-class housewives on domestic work—over seven-and-a-half hours on average per day, compared with about four hours per day spent by middle-class housewives. It would seem reasonable to interpret this difference as reflecting, at least in part, the greater use of paid servants to do domestic work in middle-class households. In 1937, therefore, there appears to have been the pattern predicted by the theory of time allocation, with greater use of formal economy provision (servants) in better-off households, and household economy provision in poorer households.

Gershuny shows that by 1961, however, the gap in domestic labour times had narrowed considerably. The main reason for this was a sharp rise in the amount of time spent on domestic work by middle-class housewives, of some 70 per cent or so over the intervening two decades. This probably reflected a reduction in the amount of domestic work performed by paid labour in middle-class households. The domestic labour time of working-class housewives, in contrast to middle-class housewives, had fallen a little over the period. This decline in working-class housewives' labour time continued during the 1960s, and middle-class housewives' domestic work time also began to decline, although less rapidly. By 1975 middle-class housewives were spending, if anything, more time on domestic work than their working-class counterparts.

It is difficult to account for these changes in housewives' domestic work times since 1937 within the framework of the theory of time allocation. The convergence and eventual reversal of the positions of middle-class and working-class housewives has meant that the pattern of domestic work time is now the opposite of that which would be predicted by the time allocation theory. It may of course be that this can be accounted for, at least to some extent, by problems with the comparability over time of the 'class' definitions used in constructing the data. In addition, the relationship between class and income differentials may have changed. Income-related differences in domestic labour time may still exist, but may no longer be adequately proxied by the difference between working-class and middle-class households.

A second factor in the convergence of labour times may have been the rising real cost of services, both as a result of a rise in the relative incomes of domestic workers and other service industry workers, and because of the slower growth in productivity of service industries. Gershuny (1983) shows that the cross-section income elasticity of demand for transport and other services fell considerably, particularly at the higher end of the income distribution, between 1959 and 1977 (p. 17). Households, he argues, are increasingly providing services for themselves, using a combination of unpaid labour and household capital goods (consumer durables), rather than purchasing final services from the formal economy. Whereas in the 1930s middle-class households found employing domestic labour preferable to spending their own time on housework, by the early 1960s the range of labour-saving equipment available had so reduced the time required for housework that own provision became a more attractive option.

The effect of higher income may now be felt more on the

technology used in household production, rather than on the division of activities between the household and formal economies. Households with higher income levels may make more use of capital-intensive, labour-saving techniques in household production (dishwashers, washing machines, food processors, etc.) than lower-income households, but both groups may perform a similar range of activities within the household economy. Time-budget data on their own may be an increasingly poor indicator of the amount of household production, both as it has changed over time and as it differs between different groups of the population. The perils of equating a reduction in labour time with a fall in output can be seen from the steady fall in the amount of time that working-class housewives spent on domestic work between 1951 and 1975, from about eight hours a day to about five-and-a-half. Probably the 'output' from their domestic work remained roughly steady, while the productivity of domestic labour time rose due to the increasing use of washing machines, electric irons, vacuum-cleaners, and other labour-saving machinery (coupled too with technological improvements in washing powders, polishes, etc. which will also have cut down domestic labour times).

'Do-it-yourself'

During the 1970s and early 1980s one of the most buoyant sectors in an otherwise slack economy has been the DIY industry. Pahl (1984, p. 101) reckons that between 1974 and 1980 consumer spending on DIY goods, tools, and home decorating grew by 19 per cent in real terms, compared with 8 per cent for all consumer spending. 'A substantial amount of production once again took place in the home by household members, which earlier in the century might have been done by employing another individual or firm.' (Pahl, 1984, p. 101.)

According to some estimates, quite an astonishing proportion of households were doing some DIY work by the early 1980s. For example, the 1981 Polycell Report (quoted by Pahl, 1984, p. 105) found that 84 per cent of adults over the age of twenty-five had painted interior woodwork during the previous twelve months, and 70 per cent had done wallpapering; 40 per cent had put up shelves, and a similar proportion had done exterior decorating and tiling. The General Household Survey, too, has found that a high percentage of the adult population does some form of DIY work. In the four weeks before the 1983 survey, 36 per cent of adults over the age of sixteen had done some DIY work (General Household Survey, 1983, p. 211). Men were roughly twice as likely to have done DIY work as women, and the frequency of DIY work was greatest (64 per cent) amongst men in the thirty to forty-four age group.

One factor behind this DIY boom, according to Pahl, has been the expansion of home-ownership, especially among lower-income groups. Certainly, spending on DIY goods appears to be significantly higher among home-owners than among tenants. An analysis of the 1983 Family Expenditure Survey shows that during the two-week survey period, 28 per cent of owner-occupiers purchased paint, DIY materials, or equipment, compared with 14 per cent of council tenants and 10 per cent of private tenants (Table 15.1). This is due partly, of course, to the fact that owner-occupiers are responsible for a far wider range of maintenance and

TABLE 15.1

Spending on Structural Additions, Repairs and Decorations, and DIY Goods, by Tenure

| | | PERCENTAGES OF HOUSEHOLDS RECORDING SPENDING ON: | | |
		Structural additions	Repairs and decorations by contractors	Paint, DIY materials, and equipment
1977	Owner-occupiers	4.3	4.5	28.8
	Council tenants	0.3	0.9	16.0
	Private tenants	0.1	1.1	14.5
1979	O	6.2	5.0	28.3
	C	0.4	1.1	14.5
	P	0.1	1.4	10.8
1981	O	8.3	4.8	28.1
	C	0.7	1.0	16.1
	P	0.6	1.5	12.2
1983	O	8.6	4.8	28.4
	C	0.8	0.5	13.7
	P	0.2	0.7	10.4

Source: Family Expenditure Survey data.

decoration tasks than tenants. Council tenants are normally responsible only for interior decoration—though of late there has been an increasing tendency for council tenants to be permitted or, occasionally, encouraged to undertake maintenance work themselves—and private tenants, especially in furnished accommodation, may not even have responsibility for interior decoration.

Table 15.1 shows a similar pattern in spending on repairs and decorations by contractors, and on structural extensions and additions. In both cases, the vast majority of spenders were owner-occupiers.

Over the period covered by Table 15.1 it is noteworthy that, in fact, the percentages of households spending on paints and DIY materials, and on repairs and decorations have remained very stable. Since 1977, therefore, there is no evidence of increasing participation in DIY work, or of an increasing number of households spending on repairs and decorations by contractors. But there was a striking growth between 1977 and 1983 in the percentage of households engaging contractors to undertake structural additions and improvements. By 1983, $8\frac{1}{2}$ per cent of owner-occupier households were spending on building works of this sort, twice as many as in 1977. Such growth had been foreseen by the industry commentators quoted by Pahl who in 1980 remarked that 'many in the trade believe that the home improvement, as opposed to DIY, boom is only now beginning in this country' (Pahl, 1984, p. 102).

Clearly, the Family Expenditure Survey (FES) data suggest an increasing use of formal economy resources in home improvement. Should this be regarded as reflecting a shift away from the informal, household economy towards the formal economy, reversing, as it were, the DIY home improvement trend observed by Pahl and others? Or is it consistent with a continuation of that trend? The answer to this question depends in part on whether DIY work should in practice be regarded as a substitute for formal economy provision in this area. It also depends on the characteristics of the households buying formal economy services and doing DIY work. To the extent that the two groups of households are very different, what appears as substitution at the aggregate level may not reflect actual substitutions at the level of individual households involved.

Table 15.2 shows the combinations of purchases made by owner-occupier households in the FES sample. The majority of the households that recorded spending on the three categories of home decoration and improvement recorded spending under only one heading. In particular, DIY materials were frequently bought by households that recorded no spending on structural additions or repairs and decorations. But there is a certain amount of evidence that all three purchase categories have a degree of complementarity; in each case, a higher percentage of the households spending on one category recorded spending on other categories than amongst the population as a whole. Thus, for example, of the 8.6 per cent of owner-occupiers spending on structural additions, about two-fifths also recorded spending on DIY materials or repairs and decorations, compared with less than a third of owner-occupiers as a whole.

TABLE 15.2

Owner-Occupiers: Purchase Combinations, 1983

	Percentage of owner-occupiers purchasing:
Structural additions only	4.7
Repairs and decorations only	2.8
DIY goods only	23.4
Structural additions, and repairs and decorations	0.4
Structural additions, and DIY goods	3.2
Repairs and decorations, and DIY goods	1.3
All three	0.3
Nothing	63.8

Source: Family Expenditure Survey data.

In the case of spending on structural additions, the complementarity is greater with purchases of DIY materials than with spending on repairs and decorations by contractors. (This, though, should be taken with caution. It may simply reflect the two-week sample used in the FES, which may be too short to contain both the payments where major work involving both structural work and decorations has been undertaken.) The complementarity appears to be least between spending on repairs and decorations and spending on DIY materials. For some households, at least, they are substitutes, and informal labour can be substituted for labour hired from the formal economy.

Table 15.3 shows how spending on structural additions, repairs and decorations, and DIY goods by owner-occupiers is related to various household characteristics: income, and the age and occupation of the head of the household. Amongst households where the head is in employment, the broad occupation category of

TABLE 15.3

Owner-Occupiers: Household Characteristics and Spending, 1983

	PERCENTAGE OF EACH CATEGORY SPENDING ON:		
	Structural additions	Repairs and decorations	DIY goods
OCCUPATION OF HEAD OF HOUSEHOLD			
Managerial/Professional	11.1	4.7	30.9
Clerical	9.5	5.4	28.6
Manual	11.3	4.8	33.8
Retired	2.4	4.1	20.8
Unoccupied	1.6	5.0	14.4
AGE OF HEAD OF HOUSEHOLD			
Under 30	8.9	4.2	34.1
30–45	11.5	4.9	32.2
45–65	9.6	4.9	29.7
Over 65	1.6	4.4	16.0
ANNUAL NORMAL INCOME (GROSS)			
Less than £3,000	0	0.5	8.0
£3,000–£5,000	1.1	5.0	15.5
£5,000–£7,000	3.6	4.1	22.5
£7,000–£9,000	6.6	3.6	25.8
Over £9,000	11.6	5.3	33.5
All owner-occupier households	8.6	4.8	28.4

Source: Family Expenditure Survey data.

the head of the household appears to have little effect on spending behaviour. Manual workers are just as likely as managerial and professional workers to pay for structural additions, or for repairs and decorations, and just as likely to purchase paint and DIY materials. More significant differences from the average can be seen in households where the head of the household is retired or 'unoccupied' (a category largely comprising the registered unemployed).

Households where the head is retired recorded spending on structural additions only about a quarter as often as the average of all owner-occupier households, and spending on DIY materials three-quarters as often. Retired households also recorded spending on contractors' repairs and decorations somewhat less frequently than average, although the difference in this category was less substantial. These differences partly reflect age; households where the head was aged over sixty-five purchased DIY materials only half as frequently as households where the head was under forty-five, and had structural additions done only one-seventh as frequently as households with a head aged between thirty and forty-five. Spending on contractors' repairs and decorations, by contrast, seems to be much less affected by age. Older people may find DIY more difficult and may tend to rely more on contractors to do repairs and decorations; they are also at a time of life when they may have little need for home extensions and may have little reason to invest further in housing assets.

'Unoccupied' households, mostly those with a head who is registered unemployed, also recorded spending much less frequently than the average on structural additions and on DIY goods. But, if anything, they were more likely to pay for contractors to do repairs and decorations. Such a pattern would seem to run counter to the usual view that the unemployed have plenty of time available to do repairs and decorations themselves. Why, when by all accounts a considerable saving can be made from DIY, do so many unemployed households appear to pay contractors to do painting and decorating, while purchasing DIY materials and equipment only half as often as the average? The process of substitution appears to be running in completely the wrong direction.

Part of the answer could be that amongst the unemployed, as amongst the retired population, there are some households that do not have the labour resources for self-provision, and are forced to fall back on purchased services for things that able-bodied people or larger households are able to do for themselves. Far from being a 'luxury', spending on repairs and decoration is less related to income than either DIY spending or spending on structural additions (which, as Table 15.3 shows, is very strongly related to income). Indeed, owner-occupier households with incomes between £3,000 and £5,000 a year appear more likely to employ builders and decorators for repairs and decorations than many higher-income households. It may indeed be that those households that have a low earning capacity in the formal economy have correspondingly little scope for productive activity within the household economy.

But, apart from some pensioner or unemployed households, there appears to be no reason that substitution between the formal economy and do-it-yourself work on home improvements and decorations should not be possible. Employing contractors to do structural additions is clearly something related very strongly to income; lower-income households may not undertake extensions at all, or may 'do-it-themselves'. But the most striking observation is that for many households contractors are used to do only part of the work; about half the households employing contractors were also buying DIY goods. Even higher-income households, while spending more often on contractors, were also the most frequent purchasers of DIY goods and, it would therefore appear, the most frequent suppliers of DIY labour.

Unemployment and the household economy

A number of commentators have taken the view that the unemployed are able to compensate for their exclusion from work in the formal economy by increasing their activity in the informal economy. Rose (1983), for example, has argued that being unemployed 'gives more time and more incentive for individuals to produce goods and services in the domestic economy to substitute for products formerly purchased in the official economy. Activities recorded in the national income accounts will increase in the former circumstances, and decrease in the latter. From the point of view of the individual, total consumption remains the same'. He sees this household production as expanding counter-cyclically to offset the decline in earnings and production in the formal economy during times of recession and high unemployment: 'when the official economy is slack, individuals can use their domestic resources to maintain consumption'.

There are a number of areas where the unemployed might be able to substitute home production for goods and services purchased from the formal economy. In many, however, the potential cost savings may be small because the economies of scale in production and in materials purchasing that formal economy producers can achieve may not be attainable in small-scale household production. Thus, for example, it may be that the savings from home-baking or home-dressmaking compared with the cheapest commercially made products are negligible. But there are some instances where significant savings can be made through home production. Home-brewing is probably the most striking example: the high levels of excise duty on alcoholic drinks mean that there are substantial savings that can be made from brewing beer at home.

The other area where the unemployed, using their own 'free' labour time, could in theory make substantial savings is in the household production of services involving a high labour input—painting and decorating, childminding, hairdressing, and so on. The scale economies attainable in formal economy production tend to be fairly low in the case of many of these activities, and while some are highly skilled—for example, plastering—many are easily undertaken within the household economy. It is, of course, an open question how many of the unemployed formerly employed cooks, nannies, or gardeners, but some serious commentators have suggested that many unemployed people may now be actively engaged in repairing, decorating, and improving their own homes using their own, free, labour time.

Further possible substitution can be envisaged if labour supply is looked at from the point of view of households, rather than individuals. An unemployed husband may be able to do more of the housework previously done by his wife, and may thereby enable his wife to work longer in the formal economy. A change in the division of labour within the household may be able partly to offset the enforced reduction in one partner's work in the formal economy.

Time-budget data in Miles (1983) provide a starting-point for a comparison of the participation of employed and unemployed men in the household economy. Table 15.4 shows Miles's comparison between the use of time by his sample of unemployed men in Brighton in 1982, and time use by full-time employed men in a national time-budget survey conducted in 1975 for the BBC. The difference in the amount of time spent on domestic work is striking. The unemployed men spent on average eight hours five minutes less per weekday in paid employment than the employed men. But the unemployed men spent nearly four hours a day on domestic work—three hours a day more than the employed men.

TABLE 15.4

Time Budgets of Employed and Unemployed Men

	Full-time employed men, UK, 1975	Unemployed men, Brighton, 1982
Time per weekday spent on:		
Paid work	8 hrs 21 mins	16 mins
Domestic work	56 mins	3 hrs 56 mins
Personal care (including sleep)	10 hrs 16 mins	9 hrs 48 mins
Civic activities	5 mins	9 mins
Leisure at home	3 hrs 4 mins	5 hrs 41 mins
Leisure away from home	1 hr 18 mins	3 hrs 20 mins

Note: The Brighton figures sum to 50 minutes less than 24 hours due to the omission of unemployment-related activities.

Source: Miles, 1983.

It should not be immediately inferred that the output of unemployed men in the household economy is four times that of employed men. Time is clearly not a scarce commodity for the unemployed; Miles notes, for example, that the growth in outdoor leisure 'really derives in large part from men going on fairly aimless walks as an alternative to utter idleness'. For some unemployed men, housework provides a structure and purpose to the day, quite apart from the output produced. Given that the time used for housework has a negligible opportunity cost, it would not be surprising if unemployed men took much longer than employed men over much the same amount of housework.

A broadly similar proportion of time was spent on domestic work by a group of unemployed Belfast men studied by Trew and Kilpatrick (1984). The authors observed that it was married men who spent most time in domestic work; one group of the unemployed in particular pursued a pattern of activity in which domestic activities featured prominently. Amongst the domestic work done, DIY activities took a considerable amount of time; on average about three-quarters of an hour a day was spent on DIY and a further quarter of an hour on gardening. About twenty minutes were spent cooking, thirty minutes doing general household chores, and nearly fifty minutes on childcare. A high proportion of the domestic work done by unemployed men would appear to be the kind of work conventionally regarded as 'men's work'; the extent to which unemployed men were performing tasks usually done by women in employed households was limited.

This conclusion is supported by Pahl's (1984) work on Sheppey. His approach focused on the performance of specific tasks, rather than on the time spent on domestic work in general. It thus has the advantage of being unaffected if the unemployed spin out domestic work to fill the time available; on the other hand, if households with an unemployed male perform certain tasks more frequently (e.g. bake cakes more often, do DIY more frequently) this will not be reflected in Pahl's measure. Pahl developed an index of the domestic division of labour, summarising the extent to which a range of household tasks were performed predominantly by one partner or the other. He found that the most important variable determining the division of labour between husband and wife is the employment status of the female partner. Households where the female partner is in full-time employment tend to share household tasks more equally than households where the female partner is employed part-time, or is a full-time housewife (Pahl, 1984, p. 270). Another influence on the domestic division of labour appeared to be the stage of the 'domestic cycle'; in households with young children the burden of household work was borne more heavily by the female partner than in households at a later stage in the domestic cycle. But the employment status of the male partner did not appear to have any marked effect on the balance of responsibility for household tasks. In households where the male partner was unemployed, the burden of household work was, if anything, borne more heavily by the female; even in the case of washing up, there was a greater likelihood that the task would be done by the woman.

Clearly, then, there is little evidence of substitution amongst members of the household if the male partner is unemployed. While unemployed men spend more time on housework, they do not appear to take over any of the tasks conventionally performed by the housewife. The suggestion that when men become unemployed they can take on some of the housework, allowing their wives to increase their labour supply in the formal economy, does not appear to correspond to what actually happens. The domestic division of labour appears to be unaffected by unemployment of the male partner, and, in addition, the wives of unemployed men are far less likely to hold full-time jobs than married women as a whole.

What evidence is there that unemployed men can usefully increase their labour supply in other spheres of the household economy apart from conventional housework? One possibility is that the unemployed might be able to increase the amount of DIY work, for example on home extensions, repairs, or improvements. Trew and Kilpatrick (1984) found that unemployed men spent on average about three-quarters of an hour a day on 'DIY activities', but it is not known how this compares with the amount of time spent by men in full-time employment.

Table 15.5 shows a further analysis of 1983 Family Expenditure Survey data on household spending on paint and other DIY equipment and materials. Households where the head of the household was unemployed purchased such goods on average about two-fifths as frequently as households where the head was in employment. Part of this difference may simply reflect income differences; unemployed households are generally poorer, and, as Table 15.3 has shown, spending on DIY goods is related to income. The evidence in Table 15.5 about this is uneven, partly no doubt because of the very small sample sizes involved. But as a broad generalisation it would appear that, for equivalent levels of 'normal' income, unemployed households spend less than their employed counterparts on DIY goods. In other words, it would appear that the temporary reduction in income suffered by unemployed households may in fact force them to reduce their spending on DIY goods. Far from being able to use their extra 'free' time to do more DIY, the expenditure data would suggest

TABLE 15.5

Unemployment and DIY Expenditures: Owner-Occupiers, 1983

| Normal household income (£ per annum) | HOUSEHOLDS RECORDING EXPENDITURE DURING SURVEY FORTNIGHT | | | | AVERAGE RECORDED SPENDING[a] | |
| | Head of household in employment | | Head of household unemployed | | Head of household in employment | Head of household unemployed |
	Per cent	Number	Per cent	Number	(£)	(£)
Under £3,000	4	1	9	9	4.19	5.85
£ 3,000–£ 5,000	21	16	7	8	10.78	13.26
£ 5,000–£ 7,000	22	48	14	9	16.51	8.22
£ 7,000–£ 9,000	25	90	27	12	8.41	18.37
£ 9,000–£11,000	32	160	17	5	27.77	4.46
£11,000–£13,000	31	135	31	5	21.84	13.93
£13,000–£15,000	36	136	22	2	22.17	1.50
Over £15,000	36	373	29	5	38.83	27.53
All households	32	959	14	55	27.75	12.47

[a] Only households recording spending.

Source: Family Expenditure Survey data.

that unemployed households reduce their spending on the goods that are needed for DIY work.

Conclusions

The three aspects of possible substitution between the formal and household economies analysed in this chapter all suggest that the boundary between the formal and household economies is relatively stable, over all except a very long time-scale. Between the 1930s and 1960s, a considerable transfer of activities took place from the formal economy to the household economy, as the number of servants employed by middle-class households declined. As a result, some activities that would have been measured in gross domestic product (GDP) at the start of the period are now being undertaken in the household economy, where they are not reflected in GDP. This transition has, however, taken place over many years, and there is no indication that the year-on-year changes in the distribution of activities between the formal and household economies have ever been sufficient for the growth rate of GDP to be a seriously misleading indicator of year-on-year changes in total economic activity.

Two areas where greater substitution might have been thought likely to take place across the boundary between the formal and household economies are DIY home improvements and the work patterns of the unemployed. In neither case, however, does it appear that economic conditions lead to substantial substitution. The amount of DIY work done does not appear to be a straightforward function of household income levels—as the time allocation model outlined in the previous chapter would suggest—and the amount of DIY work done does not appear to be explicable in terms of economic incentives alone. Even more strikingly, while unemployment leads to a rise in household working times, there appear to be both social and financial constraints on the extent of substitution of household economy work for formal economy work. Unemployed men may spend more time on certain types of household work, but they do not appear to take over any of the tasks conventionally performed by the housewife; while their ability to expand the amount of DIY work, for example, may be limited by lack of money to buy materials and equipment.

Part V
Conclusions

Chapter 16

Conclusions

The 'shadow economy', which has been the subject of this book, covers a broad spectrum of economic activity, largely unreflected in the national accounts estimates of gross domestic product and largely ignored by economic analysis. The aspect of the shadow economy that has achieved the greatest attention from the media, members of the public, and politicians alike is the 'black economy'—economic activity that is concealed from the authorities so as to evade tax or to be able to claim social security benefits to which the claimant is not in fact entitled. Because it is hidden from the eyes of the authorities, the black economy is generally not measured by official economic statistics, although the UK statistics for gross domestic product do in fact contain an allowance for concealed factor incomes—earnings and profits not declared for tax.

However, the shadow economy—in the sense in which the term has been used in this book—goes much wider than merely the productive activities of 'moonlighters' and other tax evaders. It includes also the whole range of productive activities that take place outside the formal, market economy measured in official statistics. Housework—cleaning, cooking, childcare, and so on—is only measured in the national accounts if it is performed by paid labour, and likewise the labour time devoted to do-it-yourself (DIY) home decorating and repairs is not reflected in the statistics of gross domestic product.

Scale of shadow economy activities

How great are these omissions, and how serious? Much of this book has been devoted to quantifying the black economy and other parts of the shadow economy. In Chapters 9 to 12 three major approaches to estimating the size of the black economy have been explored and evaluated. Chapter 14, on the other hand, has considered the scale of other shadow economy activities, especially housework, in relation to the formal economy.

Previous estimates of the size of the black economy in the UK have varied widely. Matthews (1983), for example, has calculated that the black economy could amount to some 15 per cent of recorded gross domestic product, while figures below 5 per cent have been suggested by both MacAfee (1980) and Dilnot and Morris (1981). It is, as Chapter 9 shows, hard to reconcile the higher estimates of black economy incomes with the actual pattern of family expenditures in the areas where the black economy is popularly believed to be rife. While some households spend large amounts on home improvements, taxis, hairdressers, and so on, the average level of household expenditures in these areas is a low percentage of total household expenditures. It might be plausible that some $2\frac{1}{2}$ per cent of household spending could be in the black economy, but for the percentage to be much higher it would be necessary for the black economy to extend far beyond those areas where most anecdotes seem to arise.

Tanzi (1982) has observed that evidence for a large black economy in the US has generally been based on analyses of monetary ratios—of the amount of cash in circulation, of trends in the circulation of high-denomination notes, and so on. Much the same is true of the UK estimates; cash methods have tended to be responsible for the high estimates of black economy activity. As Chapter 10 shows, there are grounds for serious doubt about the reliability of these methods, especially at a time when patterns of cash use have been changing rapidly for technological reasons. Different cash methods give very different answers; if some indicators show a large and rising black economy, others can be found that would suggest instead that the black economy is shrinking rapidly! This fact, if nothing else, would suggest that estimates of the size of the black economy based on selected monetary indicators should be taken with a very large pinch of salt.

If the evidence of cash indicators is to be largely discounted, what evidence remains of a massive or growing black economy? The straight answer is: not much. The discrepancy between the initial estimates of gross domestic product (GDP) based on expenditure data and on income data was suggested as an indicator of black economy incomes by MacAfee (1980). This discrepancy has, however, always been low. At its highest point in the mid-1970s it amounted to less than 5 per cent of GDP, and at present the initial estimate based on declared incomes actually exceeds the expenditure estimate. Discrepancies between spending and income at the individual household level were analysed by Dilnot and Morris (1981) using Family Expenditure Survey data. They concluded that some 10 or 15 per cent of households might have some form of concealed income, but that the total amount of hidden income was not large—perhaps $2\frac{1}{2}$ or 3 per cent of GDP.

The balance of evidence from Chapters 9 to 12 suggests that the level of black economy activity is unlikely to be less than about 3 per cent of GDP. On the other hand, even though there is reason to believe that discrepancies in the national accounts and household survey data may both tend to lead to an underestimate of black economy incomes, there is no convincing evidence that the black economy in the UK approaches anything like 15 per cent of GDP. Even 5 per cent would seem a high, though not inconceivable, upper bound.

As Dilnot and Morris (1981) observed, the black economy can quite easily be large enough to yield a rich vein of anecdotes without necessarily being a phenomenon of quantitative significance. While the popular view that tax evasion is rife receives little support from these results, it does appear that there may be a problem of a substantial level of tax evasion amongst certain groups of the population. One aspect, explored in Chapter 12, is the relative standards of living of employees and the self-employed at similar levels of declared income. Comparisons of spending patterns suggest that self-employed incomes might be understated, relative to employee incomes, by some 10 to 20 per cent—much the level of tax evasion by the self-employed that is in fact assumed by the compilers of the UK national accounts.

The problems of measuring the black economy stem largely from the concealment of incomes from the tax authorities and, in consequence, from statisticians and economic researchers too. The problems of measuring other components of the shadow economy are different. As Chapter 14 describes, the main obstacle to measuring unpaid productive activities such as housework and DIY is the lack of market prices to form the basis of a valuation of the outputs produced. One approach, adopted by a number of researchers in the US, has been to value the output of housework by valuing the unpaid labour time involved in household production. However, there are problems with such an approach; in particular, it is by no means clear that any satisfactory basis exists for valuing the substantial amounts of time that people typically devote to housework.

On the other hand, while it may be difficult to devise a method of valuing the output of the household economy in a way that is directly comparable with the formal economy measured in GDP, it is nonetheless clear that the household economy is substantial. Survey evidence from 'time-budget' data suggests that almost as many hours may be devoted to work in the household economy as to paid work in the formal economy—despite the great improvements in productivity in the household economy in recent years, through the development of labour-saving appliances and materials.

Policy implications

Overall, then, it would appear that, while the black economy is small in relation to economic activity in the formal economy, the household economy is considerably larger. To what extent would it be true to summarise the situation by saying that the household economy is large, but not a problem, while the black economy is small, yet is a problem?

There are, in fact, a number of policy issues that are common to the various parts of the shadow economy. One question, raised immediately by our estimates of the size of the shadow economy, is its implications for the economic statistics that are used to guide macroeconomic policy. Some have argued, for example, that many of the registered unemployed are actively employed in the black economy—with the clear implication that too much is being made of the problem of unemployment. More generally, the signals that the national accounts statistics give about the rate of growth of the economy, about the pressure of demand, and about other aspects of economic performance may have been positively misleading. Mistaken policies may have been the consequence of statistical illusions (Gutmann, 1979b) caused by ignoring the black economy or other aspects of economic activity not recorded in the national accounts. In charting our macroeconomic course, have we ended up steering the ship by the wrong stars?

Undoubtedly, the black economy gives rise to problems for the statisticians who compile the national accounts. The fact that some economic activity is being consciously concealed from the tax authorities means that some potential data sources are seriously contaminated by evasion. But, as Chapter 11 has shown, the UK national accounts are the product of accounting relationships, with considerable scope for cross-checking between information from different data sources. Indeed, this cross-checking provides the basis for the estimates of the size of the black economy by MacAfee (1980), and allows some of the more unreliable data inputs to the national accounts to be systematically adjusted for the effects of tax evasion.

Nevertheless, while the possibilities for cross-checking in the national accounts mean that it is unlikely that massive swings in the amount of black economy activity would go unnoticed, there are some more insidious threats to the accuracy of the accounts. Most data sources, not just the income data from tax returns, might be affected to a greater or lesser extent by the black economy, and so a reliable yardstick for cross-checking may not exist. Cross-checking procedures and improvements to estimation methods may eliminate discrepancies, but may not ensure accuracy. However, to remain undetected this process could only be a gradual one, and would not invalidate the usefulness of the national accounts statistics as indicators of year-to-year changes in activity.

What is at issue here is the extent of substitution between the formal and shadow economies, rather than the absolute size of either. The occasional calls for a 'new national accounts', including shadow economy activities, may have some point if the national accounts are used to compare living standards across countries, for example. But in their primary application, as indicators of short-term changes in economic activity, absolute levels of GDP are less relevant than changes in GDP. These would only be poorly estimated if there was substantial instability in the border-line between the formal and shadow economies, with considerable transfers of activities from one to the other. From Chapters 9 to 12 for the black economy and Chapters 14 and 15 for the wider shadow economy, there is no evidence of substitution between the formal and shadow economies on a scale sufficient to undermine the value of the national accounts as indicators of the state of the economy.

Substitution, too, is the point at issue in assessing the

implications of the shadow economy for tax policy. High levels of taxation may provide an incentive to seek ways of avoiding taxation, either in the black economy, or outside the framework of the money economy altogether through do-it-yourself or voluntary work. Such substitutions are inherently inefficient, in that they involve people choosing ways of doing things that they would not choose in the absence of taxation. Inefficient firms evading tax may be able to undercut their efficient, but honest, competitors. Economic resources may thus be wasted, by being employed less efficiently. The objective of policy must be to minimise this waste, subject to satisfying the revenue needs of the State.

Policy can operate in a number of different ways. Tax rates themselves might be altered, to reduce the rates of taxation in areas where the greatest distortions of activity were arising, and to increase taxation in areas where distortions were less of a problem. Changes to tax structure or administration might be considered, to reduce the opportunities for tax evasion or for other substitutions between the formal and shadow economy in sensitive areas. There is also the issue of enforcement.

House maintenance, repair, and decoration stands out as an area of economic activity where the scope for formal economy / shadow economy substitution is particularly high. Indirect taxation of these activities in the formal economy is relatively recent, dating from the introduction of value added tax (VAT) a little over a decade ago. The sharp rise in taxation and the lack of any tradition of taxpaying in the industry may have been factors that contributed to a high level of black economy business in the industry. But more important factors perhaps, as discussed in Chapter 6, are the high level of sales to private individuals and the small-scale nature of many businesses. The low capital and modest skill requirements of many house maintenance, repair, and decoration activities have also contributed both to a degree of informality in the market provision of these services and to a high level of self-provision through DIY.

Steps have already been taken to control some aspects of tax evasion in building and construction—for example, by the special provisions for the taxation of labour-only subcontractors. Payments made to labour-only subcontractors can be subject to tax deduction at source, in much the same way as employees are taxed through Pay-As-You-Earn (PAYE). Further, more radical steps might be taken in this area, particularly if it were felt that tax evasion in building and decorating businesses was undermining a more general acceptance of taxpaying morality. One possibility that might be considered is to impose a much greater obligation than at present on customers of these services to ensure that tax has been paid. This might be done, for example, by requiring householders who were having extensive building and maintenance work done (say, valued at over £2,000) to notify the Inland Revenue and to deduct tax at source. Such a move would, of course, be unlikely to eliminate the black economy entirely, since there would still be scope for mutual financial gain from concealment. But concealment would involve the customer, as well as the supplier, in law-breaking, and would thus add significantly to the risks borne by customers in the black economy. In some cases this might help to tip the balance in favour of formal economy suppliers rather than their moonlighting competitors.

As far as the administration of income tax is concerned, the Keith Committee (1983) made a number of recommendations designed to encourage people with casual sources of income to declare them for tax. One recommendation that has not been acted on is to ensure that all taxpayers are asked explicitly whether they have sources of casual income to declare. At the moment only a minority of taxpayers are actually issued with a tax return; in these circumstances it is difficult to complain if many taxpayers fail to declare black economy sources of income to the Inland Revenue.

The option of greater enforcement effort is one that should be pursued selectively. It is not possible in this area to accept the view that the law should be enforced merely because it is the law. There are always the questions of costs and benefits, and the appropriate direction of marginal resources. It is likely that there are some areas where the economic losses from enforcement are greater than elsewhere: as Chapter 4 has observed, in areas where labour supply is highly elastic it may be desirable to 'go easy' on enforcement, to minimise the economic costs of the tax system. Of course, identifying such areas of elastic labour supply is by no means straightforward. One area, however, where the output losses from rigorous enforcement might plausibly be expected to be high would be in the taxation of casual earnings from baby-sitting and other small-scale activities. The fact that in these areas the resource costs of enforcement work might in any case be high in relation to the tax recovered would provide a further reason for turning a blind eye to some level of evasion.

What, in any case, are the costs of *not* enforcing the tax system? In the short term at least, the cost is merely the cost of raising revenue elsewhere, through a higher level of general taxation: in other words, the marginal resource costs of public funds. Topham (1984) calculates that the marginal resource cost of each additional pound raised through income taxation is £1.21, i.e. the pound raised, plus twenty-one pence 'excess burden' reflecting the distorting and disincentive effects of taxation. Enforcement is only worthwhile (in the sense of raising revenue at lower resource cost) if the costs of raising a pound through enforcement are less than this. The cost:yield ratios for enforcement work discussed in Chapters 7 and 8 are in fact not far out of line from the 1:5 ratio of costs to yield that would be the minimum justifiable on this basis. Assuming diminishing returns to enforcement, therefore, there would not seem to be any strong case on resource grounds for increasing the present broad level of resources devoted to enforcement.

But this short-term perspective can be dangerous. Money spent on enforcement now may not only recover tax this year, but may also ensure better compliance in future years. Deterrence, as well as cost-effective tax recovery, should be the objective of enforcement policy, and well-publicised and visible prosecutions may, in the long term, do more good than low-key agreements to recover unpaid tax. This is all the more important in view of the strong sense of fairness that seems to underpin many taxpayers' attitudes to the tax system. Surveys such as Miller (1979), for example, appear to suggest that people's willingness to comply with the tax system is strongly influenced by whether they think other people are complying too. 'I don't see why I should pay all my tax when others don't' seems to be a not uncommon view.

From this standpoint, of course, anecdotal accounts of the black economy, and the publicity given to wild and improbable estimates of its size, are not merely innocuous entertainment, but are profoundly damaging. It would be bad enough if we were ever to get to the point where tax was being widely evaded on such a massive scale that an acceptance of tax evasion became the norm. But for people's willingness to pay tax to be undermined by an incorrect perception of the actual level of evasion would be a needless irony. The evidence in this book does not suggest that the black economy is particularly large or that the tax system in general is close to break-down. Undoubtedly problems of enforcement do exist in some areas; but their solution will rarely be made any easier by continuing misapprehension of the actual scale of the black economy.

Bibliography

Alden, J., 'Holding two jobs: an examination of "moonlighting"', pp. 43-57 in Henry, S. (ed.), *Can I Have It In Cash?*, London, Astragal Books (1981).

Allen, D. and Hunn, A., 'An evaluation of the Enterprise Allowance Scheme', *Employment Gazette*, vol. 93, no. 8, pp. 313-17 (August 1985).

Allingham, M. G. and Sandmo, A., 'Income tax evasion: a theoretical analysis', *Journal of Public Economics*, vol. 1, no. 3/4, pp. 323-38 (1972).

Atkinson, A. B. and Micklewright, J., 'On the reliability of income data in the Family Expenditure Survey 1970-77', Social Science Research Council Programme on Taxation, Incentives and the Distribution of Income, Discussion Paper no. 40 (1982).

Bank of England, 'Recent changes in the use of cash', *Bank of England Quarterly Bulletin*, vol. 22, no. 4, pp. 519-29 (1984).

Becker, G. S., 'A theory of the allocation of time', *Economic Journal* (September 1965).

Beveridge Report, *Social Insurance and Allied Services*, Report by Sir William Beveridge, Cmd 6404, London, HMSO (1942).

Blades, D., *The Hidden Economy and the National Accounts*, OECD Economic Outlook, Occasional Studies, Paris, OECD (1982).

Brown, C. V., Levin, E. J., Rosa, P. J., and Ulph, D. T., 'Tax evasion and avoidance on earned income: some survey evidence', *Fiscal Studies*, vol. 5, no. 3, pp. 1-22 (1984).

Bullock, N., Dickens, P., Shapcott, M., and Steadman, P., 'Time budgets and models of urban activity patterns', *Social Trends*, no. 5, pp. 45-63 (1974).

Cagan, P., 'The demand for currency relative to total money supply', *Journal of Political Economy* (August 1958).

Central Statistical Office, 'United Kingdom national accounts: sources and methods', third edition, Studies in Official Statistics no. 37, London, HMSO (1985).

Clark, C., 'The economics of housework', *Bulletin of the Oxford Institute of Statistics*, pp. 205-11 (May 1958).

Coffield, F., Borrill, C., and Marshall, S., 'How young people try to survive being unemployed', *New Society*, pp. 332-4 (2 June 1983).

Cowell, F. A., 'The economics of tax evasion: a survey', Economic and Social Research Council Programme on Taxation, Incentives and the Distribution of Income, Discussion Paper no. 80 (July 1985).

Deane, K. D., 'Tax evasion, criminality, and sentencing the tax offender', *British Journal of Criminology*, vol. 21, no. 1 (1981).

Department of Health and Social Security, *Evaluation of Specialist Claims Control and Comparison with Other Types of Anti-Fraud Work: Summary Report* (1985).

Dilnot, A. W. and Morris, C. N., 'What do we know about the black economy?', *Fiscal Studies*, vol. 2, no. 1, pp. 58–73 (1981).

——, Kay, J. A., and Morris, C. N., *The Reform of Social Security*, Oxford University Press (1984a).

——, Kay, J. A., and Morris, C. N., 'The UK tax system, structure and progressivity, 1948–82', *Scandinavian Journal of Economics*, vol. 86, no. 2, pp. 150–65 (1984b).

Feige, E. L., 'How big is the irregular economy?', *Challenge*, no. 22, pp. 5–13 (November/December 1979).

——, 'A new perspective on macroeconomic phenomena—the theory and measurement of the unobserved sector of the United States economy: causes, consequences and implications', presented at the ninety-third Annual Meeting of the American Economic Association (September 1980).

——, 'The UK's unobserved economy: a preliminary assessment', *Journal of Economic Affairs*, vol. 1, no. 4, pp. 205–12 (1981).

——, 'The meaning of the "underground economy" and the full compliance deficit', in Gaertner, W. and Wenig, A., *The Economics of the Shadow Economy: Proceedings of the International Conference on the Economics of the Shadow Economy held at the University of Bielefeld, West Germany, October 10–14, 1983*, Berlin, Springer-Verlag (1985).

—— and McGee, R. T., 'Tax revenue losses and the unobserved economy in the UK', *Journal of Economic Affairs*, vol. 2, no. 3, pp. 164–71 (1982).

Ferman, L. A. and Berndt, L. E., 'The irregular economy', pp. 26–42 in Henry, S. (ed.), *Can I Have It In Cash?*, London, Astragal Books (1981).

Fisher Committee, *Committee of Inquiry into the Abuse of Social Security Benefits*, Cmnd 5228, London, HMSO (1973).

Freud, D., 'A guide to underground economics', *Financial Times*, p. 16 (9 April 1979).

Gershuny, J. I., *Social Innovation and the Division of Labour*, Oxford University Press (1983).

—— and Pahl, R. E., 'Work outside employment: some preliminary speculations', *New Universities Quarterly*, vol. 34, no. 1, pp. 120–5 (1979). Reprinted in Henry, S. (ed.), *Can I Have It In Cash?*, London, Astragal Books (1981).

Greenberg, J., 'Avoiding tax avoidance: a (repeated) game-theoretic approach', *Journal of Economic Theory*, vol. 32, pp. 1–13 (1984).

Gutmann, P. M., 'The subterranean economy', *Financial Analysts Journal*, pp. 26–7,34 (November–December 1977).

——, 'The grand unemployment illusion', *Journal of the Institute for Socioeconomic Studies*, vol. 4, no. 2, pp. 20–9 (1979a).

——, 'Statistical illusions, mistaken policies', *Challenge*, no. 22, pp. 14–17 (November/December 1979b).

Hawrylyshyn, O., 'The value of household services: a survey of empirical estimates', *Review of Income and Wealth*, series 22, no. 2, pp. 101–31 (1976).

——, 'Towards a definition of non-market activities', *Review of Income and Wealth*, May, pp. 79–96 (1977).

Henry, S., 'The working unemployed: perspectives on the informal economy and unemployment', *The Sociological Review*, vol. 30, no. 3, pp. 460–77 (1982).

Hill, T. P., 'Do-it-yourself and GDP', *Review of Income and Wealth*, vol. 25, no. 1, pp. 31–9 (1979).

House of Commons Expenditure Committee, *Administration of Inland Revenue: Minutes of Evidence*, HC 312-i, Session 1978/9, London, HMSO (26 March 1979).

Inter-Bank Research Organisation, 'Consumer payments and financial behaviour', IBRO Research Brief (1982).

Johnston, R. B., 'The demand for non-interest bearing money in the United Kingdom', Government Economic Service Working Paper no. 66, London, HM Treasury (1984).

Kay, J. A. and King, M. A., *The British Tax System*, third edition, Oxford University Press (1983).

Keenan, A. and Dean, P. N., 'Moral evaluations of tax evasion', *Social Policy and Administration*, vol. 14, no. 3, pp. 209–20 (1980).

Keith Committee, *Committee on Enforcement Powers of the Revenue Departments*, Report, vols 1 and 2, Cmnd 8822, London, HMSO (1983).

Kolm, S.-C., 'A note on optimum tax evasion', *Journal of Public Economics*, vol. 2, pp. 265–70 (1973).

Lancaster, K. J., 'A new approach to consumer theory', *Journal of Political Economy*, vol. 74, pp. 132–57 (1966).

MacAfee, K., 'A glimpse of the hidden economy in the national accounts', *Economic Trends*, no. 316, pp. 81–7 (February 1980).

Mars, G. and Nicod, M., 'Hidden rewards at work: the implications from a study of British hotels', pp. 58–72 in Henry, S. (ed.), *Can I Have It In Cash?*, London, Astragal Books (1981).

Matthews, K., 'National income and the black economy', *Economic Affairs*, pp. 261–7 (July 1983).

—— and Rastogi, A., 'Little Mo and the moonlighters: another look at the black economy', Liverpool Research Group in Macroeconomics, *Quarterly Economic Bulletin*, vol. 6, no. 2 (1985).

Maurice, R. (ed.), *National Accounts Statistics: Sources and Methods*, London, HMSO (1968).

Miles, I., 'Adaptation to unemployment?', University of Sussex, Science Policy Research Unit, Occasional Paper Series no. 20 (1983).

Miller, R., 'Evidence of attitudes to evasion from a sample survey', in Seldon, A. (ed.), *Tax Avoision*, London, Institute of Economic Affairs (1979).

O'Higgins, M., *Measuring the Hidden Economy: A Review of Evidence and Methodologies*, Outer Circle Policy Unit (1980).

Pahl, R. E., *Divisions of Labour*, Oxford, Basil Blackwell (1984).

Peacock, A. and Shaw, G. K., 'Is tax revenue loss overstated?', *Journal of Economic Affairs*, vol. 2, no. 3, pp. 161–3 (1982).

Phelps Brown Committee, *Report of the Committee of Inquiry into Certain Matters Concerning Labour in Building and Civil Engineering*, Cmnd 3714, London, HMSO (1968).

Public Accounts Committee, 'Minutes of evidence taken before the Committee of Public Accounts, Wednesday 9 March 1983', PAC 160-iii, Session 1982/3, London, HMSO (1983).

Reinganum, J. F. and Wilde, L. L., 'Sequential equilibrium detection and reporting policies in a model of tax evasion', California Institute of Technology, Social Science Working Paper no. 525 (1984).

Reuter, P., 'The irregular economy and the quality of macroeconomic statistics', pp. 125–43 in Tanzi, V. (ed.), *The Underground Economy in the United States and Abroad*, Massachusetts, Lexington (1982).

Rose, R., 'Getting by in three economies: the resources of the official, unofficial and domestic economies', University of Strathclyde, Centre for the Study of Public Policy, Studies in Public Policy no. 110 (1983).

Ross, I., 'Why the underground economy is booming', *Fortune*, no. 98, pp. 92–9 (9 October 1978).

Sandmo, A., 'Income tax evasion, labour supply and the equity–efficiency tradeoff', *Journal of Public Economics*, vol. 16, no. 3, pp. 265–88 (1981).

Singh, B., 'Making honesty the best policy', *Journal of Public Economics*, vol. 2, pp. 257–63 (1973).

Srinivasan, T. N., 'Tax evasion: a model', *Journal of Public Economics*, vol. 2, pp. 339–46 (1973).

Tanzi, V., 'Underground economy and tax evasion in the United States: estimates and implications', Banca Nazionale del Lavoro, *Quarterly Review* (December 1980).

——, 'A second (and more skeptical) look at the underground economy in the United States', in Tanzi, V. (ed.), *The Underground Economy in the United States and Abroad*, Massachusetts, Lexington (1982).

Topham, N., 'A reappraisal and recalculation of the marginal cost of public funds', *Public Finance*, vol. 34, no. 3 (1984).

Trew, K. and Kilpatrick, R., *The Daily Life of the Unemployed: Social and Psychological Dimensions*, Queen's University of Belfast, Department of Psychology (1984).

US Internal Revenue Service, *Estimates of Income Unreported on Individual Income Tax Returns*, Publication no. 1104, Washington DC, Government Printing Office (1979).